Taking CHANCES

Also by the Author

Quitting

Taking
CHANCES

Lessons in Putting
Passion and Creativity
Into Your Work Life

Dale Dauten

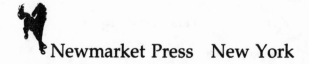
Newmarket Press   New York

This book published simultaneously in the United States of America and in Canada.

First Edition
1 2 3 4 5 6 7 8 9 0

Library of Congress Cataloging-in-Publication Data

Dauten, Dale A.
  Taking chances.

  Bibliography: p.
  1. Success in business.   2. Career development.
I. Title.
HF5386.D214   1986   331.7'02   85-43240
ISBN: 0-937858-70-6

Quantity Purchases
Companies, professional groups, clubs, and other organizations may qualify for special terms when ordering quantities of this title. For information, contact the Special Sales Department, Newmarket Press, 18 East 48th Street, New York, N.Y. 10017. Phone (212) 832-3575.

Designed by Susan Brooker/Levavi and Levavi

Manufactured in the United States of America

To
Ruth Cavin
who took the first chance
on this writer

No man ever yet became great by imitation.

Samuel Johnson

CONTENTS

Acknowledgments   xi

Introduction: The Line   1

Part One: Wealths   13
    Chapter 1: The Tune   17
    Chapter 2: Your Map of the Future   39

Part Two: Purposeful Career Crafting   63
    Chapter 3: The Explorer   65
    Chapter 4: The Idea Ranch   89

Part Three: Implementation   149
    Chapter 5: Paints and Brushes   151
    Chapter 6: Striking Matches   169

Bibliography   191

ACKNOWLEDGMENTS

A decade ago, a professional hypnotist claimed to have determined that I was a trial lawyer in my previous life. Despite my efforts to dismiss this bit of foolishness, it has stuck with me. Among other things, it offers an explanation for my obsession with asking questions, especially the tough ones. Which brings me to the particular joy of authoring this book: it gave me so many questions to ask of those I admire. The pages that follow will make apparent the intellectual generosity of many to whom my questions were put. On the other hand, the particular sorrow of authoring this book is that so many marvelous answers had to be, for one reason or another, left out. The words of some of those who were most helpful and most wise appear but briefly in the final text; this is particularly true of Harry Wolf, Roger Myers, Fred Rentschler, Steve Brown, Chris Rex, Andreas Brown, and Davis Masten. And others who made significant contributions are not directly quoted: Durwood McAlister, Martin Platt, Phil Atkins-Pattenson, Richard Protovin, Jim Murtagh, Manning Pynn, and Conley Ingram. I hope each will nevertheless recognize his influence glimmering through my text.

As for the actual bringing forth of this book, it was Peter Fleming who gave me the gumption to undertake it and who had the sense to bring me together with Esther Margolis and her Newmarket Press. (I regret that I was unable to persuade Esther to let me include her career story in this book—she will make publishing history before she hangs up her book jacket.)

My warmest thanks also go to those who helped me turn a filing cabinet full of notes and interviews and background articles into finished text—Shari Butler, Emabeth Pinella, Randy Farhi, and, above all, my charming, faithful editor, Kathy Heintzelman, from whom I learned much.

And finally, my thanks to the large-hearted friends who gave of their energies to help this book—Robert Dunn, Jud Moore, Katherine Madden, Lucy O'Brien, Bruce Brittain, Darrell Ray, John Yow, and, especially, Davis Masten and Michaela O'Brien. What riches I possess in friends such as these.

INTRODUCTION

THE LINE

Toto, I've a feeling we aren't in Kansas anymore.

Dorothy in *The Wizard of Oz*

Every bit as well as I remember buying my first car or sneaking my first kiss, I recall my first corporate hug. The company president had just uttered that thrilling cliché, "I could use you on my team," when he strode around his great oak desk, put his burly arm across my grateful shoulders and squeezed, adding, "Pay attention to my style; I'm grooming you."

That, I submit, was the *end* of my career as a corporate executive. For I heeded that presidential advice—study him I did, *imitate* him I did ... with decreasing zeal and increasing alarm. Something was wrong, dreadfully wrong. Here's the incident that convinced me:

My mentor's machismo image sprang from a management style that could best be described as Stalinistic. For instance: waving me into a chair as he instructed his secretary to call a meek, failing district manager in Wisconsin, he next snatched up the phone and without a "howdydo" set about bellowing and swearing and even, after announcing, "I'm gonna kick this phone 'cause I can't reach your ass," throwing the phone down and stomping on it.

Determined to succeed by imitation, I wanted to give it a try. Here was the rub: I couldn't bring myself to scream obscenities at a subordinate. Nevertheless, I so coveted the appellation "a man's man" that I connived to be thought ruthless. One day when three peers were chatting in the hallway outside my office, I picked up the phone and shouted insults at the dial tone, then beat the handset against my desk. A man!

This transpired in the mid-seventies; that old Zen conundrum, "the sound of one hand clapping," still echoed in my ears. Remember it? How about, "It's what you *are* that counts, not what you *have*," and the others: personal freedom, spontaneity, self-actualization. Some of you may still believe such childish notions. I did. Still do. Which is why I walked in and told the president I quit.

All I knew to do was to go to another company, one with more likable role models. So I did, this time with one of the country's giant conglomerates. But I was never the same after that first corporate hug—I kept picturing myself as president. And guess what I saw? One dull job. Twenty years of sacrifice, luck, and achievement, and maybe, just maybe, I would move to the head of the conference table . . . same tedious meetings, same blurry printouts of nums and figs (that's "numbers and figures" to those of you who don't speak corporatese), same weary, wary lifestyle.

Perplexed, I took a vacation alone—for the first time before or since. On a Mexican beach I tried to puzzle out what had gone wrong. Here I was, still in my mid-twenties, a closet student of Dale Carnegie and Napoleon Hill (I was too "intellectual" to read such books openly), an expert on fitting in, a man on the "fast track." And I wanted none of it. I had found security when adventure was what I craved. I had learned to imitate when I yearned to create. In the silent heat of Mexico I heard a small voice of self-reliance, what Emerson described this way:

> These are the voices which we hear in solitude, but they grow faint and inaudible as we enter into the world. Society everywhere is in conspiracy against the manhood of every one of its members. Society is a joint-stock company, in which the members agree, for the better securing of his bread to each shareholder, to surrender the liberty and culture of the eater. The virtue in most request is conformity. Self-reliance is its adversion.

If Emerson is a bit too remote for your taste, here's Humphrey Bogart as a con on the lam in *Desperate Hours*:

> I kinda like takin' chances. You don't take chances, you might as well be dead.

5

TAKING CHANCES

All the "fast track" and "career path" books ever published were of no use to me—I sought no track, wanted off the path. I guess you could say that there in Mexico I started writing this book, a book for impatient, self-reliant folk who like taking chances. It was there in Mexico, a decade ago, that I realized that every book on achievement I'd ever read had a basic flaw.

Let me explain that last remark . . .

Uncommon Denominators

Consider the hundreds, probably thousands of books that have looked accomplishment in the eye and reported on what they saw. What have they found? Where do they agree?

Each author set out to identify *common denominators* of success. Each author found a few and offered them for sale. But this very "common denominator" process is defective. Discover the flaw for yourself.

Think of the last five presidents. What do they have in common?

Ambition? Of course; that's like saying successful accountants can add. But compare their backgrounds, their styles, their philosophies, their faces. The antitheses shout down the theses. Further, this presidential exercise is a simple one—imagine trying to define common traits among careers as diverse as ballet dancer, architect, journalist, and corporate executive. Impossible.

Every writer on achievement has made the same fundamental mistake, that of searching for common denominators. In hoping to get a snapshot of suc-

cess, they ignore its motion—they build model air-
planes but never learn to fly. *The true distinguishing
factor of achievement is being uncommon*—a common
denominator to end all common denominators.

Like the members of any group, the successful do
have shared traits, but the commonalities are, or
might as well be, coincidental—for what makes a
person great is what he shares with no one. People
make their lives into original works of art because of
what each does *differently*. The will to be unique is
the soul of accomplishment.

Different is not always better, but better is always different. You can't be better by being the
same.

Sounds obvious, doesn't it? Harry Wolf, a man
who has been called one of America's greatest living
architects, urged me not to be afraid of such simplicity: "You know you've heard the truth," he said,
"when your reaction is to snap your fingers and say,
'I knew that—I just didn't *know* I knew that.'"

You can't be better by being the same. Yet in every
corporation in America the brightest, most ambitious
young executives are trying to surpass their peers by
doing exactly what every one of their peers is doing,
emulating the chairman, being an imitation. Like
conductors imitating Bernstein or boxers imitating
Ali. All trying to be better by being the same.

This is not a refusal to learn from the achievements of others, far from it—much of this book is
devoted to understanding how genius is borrowed—
but I am suggesting that when a person imitates, he
gets into a line. The longest lines are those emulat-

ing writers of success books. There are tens of millions of "Good Scout" executives all imitating Carnegie or Peale or Mandino. And all are ... slowly ... succeeding, for they are the new middle class. Another line is the power/intimidation one. There are fewer people in that line because it's so unpleasant there. And there's the Japanese line. It's already getting crowded. And the best to be hoped for in the Japanese line, *in any line*, is to be an imitation, a mass-produced reproduction.

To remember that, I wrote myself a fable.

THE LINE
A Fable

The lad called Swift packed his new diploma among his meager belongings and left the dormitory. With many sad glances over his shoulder, Swift went out into the world. He wandered for many days until at last he came upon a great crowd. The crowd was in fact a long, wide line of men and women with anxious expressions. Even as he looked on, mouth agape, the line grew. There was continual commotion—pushing and shoving. The lad jumped in, elbows out. After standing a long while, he tried to strike up a conversation with those around him. "Where does the line lead?" he asked the woman just ahead of him. "Shhh," she hissed. But when she looked into his innocent face, she added softly, "I don't know where it goes."

"I know," said the man ahead of her. "It goes to the grand mansion on the hill. Look, you can see it on the horizon. It is the house of the privileged few. Admittance is limited, of course; otherwise it wouldn't be the house of the privileged few. Someday I will dwell there."

This news pleased Swift. He was glad to have

found the right line so soon after leaving the dormitory. He waited. Alas, the lad waited and waited but the line did not seem to move. "What do you do here to pass the time?" Swift asked the man. "Worry," he said. "We worry about who might crowd into line and about keeping our suits pressed and our breath fresh . . . just in case."

"I'm not certain I can stand that," the lad suggested, his brow furrowed.

"Just stand awhile . . . you'll get used to it," the man replied. "Besides, we should get a new story soon."

"A story?"

"When they let someone enter the mansion, the word will travel back to us. It will come as if on a wave. You'll see. And you will take heart. The stories are so inspiring! We often weep at their telling."

So, Swift waited, although he shifted and stretched and restlessness traveled where his blood should have. He was most discouraged. New people were getting behind him and thus the line seemed to move, but did it? He could not be certain.

At last he could wait no longer and his legs carried him away. As he left the line those who saw him do so shook their heads and felt sorry for him. Some even made jokes at his expense.

As Swift wandered along, many in line gave him evil looks. Some called him names. Others advised him: "Get back in the line before it is too late." He noticed that as he moved forward along the line, the people were older and older. Finally, over gray heads, he saw the rusty gates to the mansion. Those near the gates gave counsel to those behind them. All the gray heads nodded seriously.

Swift let despair into his hopeful heart: "What a long trip!" he moaned, holding his head. "One step a year makes a city block a lifelong journey!" he cried to the jays in the trees.

The jays voiced their own complaints and flew off. With nothing else to do, he followed their direction, walking along the fence.

He had been walking awhile when he saw the end of the fence come into view. It stopped near the back door of the mansion. There he found the door open. His heart leaping into his throat, he walked inside.

"Welcome!" a dozen voices said in unison. "Come in, come in," they were all saying, offering him beverages and chairs. He sat. "Welcome home!" one said, squeezing the lad's hand.

"I can stay?" asked Swift.

"Of course. You've arrived."

"But what about those in line?"

"They will wait."

The moral?

You can't be different by being the same.

Conventional security and conventional success go to the conventional, to those who wait in line. Great accomplishment (or failure) goes only to those who get out of line. Agreed?

If so, we are ready for some adventure. Believing in getting out of line is the start, but only that—a man asleep in the gutter is also a man out of line. Here's what else we must accomplish:

1. Each day, beginning with the first day of school, a child is unconsciously and consciously trained to get in line: "Sit down! Be careful! Patience!" I am going to try to deprogram you, to teach you to hear the small voice inside you. I am going to invite you to be accomplished and free, more than rich.

2. Every book on accomplishment ever written has offered a template, a mold into which each reader is encouraged to pour his or her life. None of that for us. If you are going to be accomplished and free, more than rich, you must learn to *make molds*, to invent a style all your own.

This book is divided into two sections that correspond to these two goals. Expect some work. My aim is that no two readers will see in this book the same vision, take from it the same conclusions. It offers not a new line, but a way out of lines. If you don't take chances you might as well be dead.

PART
ONE

Wealths

THOSE OF US ADULTS BORN AFTER WORLD WAR II, THE BABY Boomers, are children of Positive Thinkers, raised in the Era of Unlimited Possibilities. We intellectually suckled on "Whatever the mind of man can conceive and believe, it can achieve." None of this "low self-esteem" stuff for us. Ask college-bound high school seniors to evaluate their talents in comparison to their peers, and you'll hear this: 70 percent rate their "leadership" abilities as above average, while just 2 percent call themselves below average; 60 percent place themselves in the top 10 percent in "ability to get along with others," with 25 percent immodestly choosing the top 1 percent. I'm O.K. You're O.K.

Never has a generation had such high expectations. We were the first generation *expected* to graduate from college. And we did—nearly twenty million of us since 1960, the largest glut of educated labor in the history of the paycheck. Hard work. Ambition. Money.

But along the way we also absorbed the message of the hippies, giving us another set of expectations: the brotherhood of man, spontaneity, individuality.

So where does that leave us? We are the *Expectations Generation*—twenty million of us crowded into line for success.

Never have so many asked so much: freedom and individuality, as well as status and wealth. And be quick about it. But you cannot march in line and still stop to smell the roses: virtually all my fellow Baby Boomers have already traded "freedom and individuality" for a shot at "status and wealth," rationalizing that upon achieving the latter goals they can purchase the former. But even with that compromise, nearly all will fail, for wealth and status are relative—only ten percent get to be in the top ten percent. I suppose you think you're a future ten-percenter. Don't forget: the *majority* of our generation thinks they're that good. But whether or not you're ten-percent or one-percent caliber is, I submit, irrelevant. There are more important questions to be answered.

CHAPTER 1

THE
TUNE

---■---

You ain't callin' the tune. I got my guts full
of you shiny-shoes, down-your-nose wise guys
with white handkerchiefs in your pockets.

Humphrey Bogart in *Desperate Hours*

It is the fashion among writers of non-fiction to pad the front of a book, putting as much interesting material there as possible . . . the literary equivalent of silicone injections. The assumption is, you see, what with all the distractions of modern life, readers will give a book only about thirty pages before making a decision about finishing it.

Forgive me then, good but harried reader, if I try your patience for a few pages and introduce here, so near your read-or-not-to-read decision, what will be the most challenging part of this book. We must, before going any further, ask ourselves, "What is success?" I can see your eyes glazing over as if I had just asked "What is love?" or some other question too vague to be diverting. But if you get out of line, you must set your own course, you must pick a star to follow.

Arnold Mitchell of SRI International, a major think-tank/research center (formerly called Stanford Research Institute), offered a list of status symbols—past, present, and future—for the type of person he called the Achiever:

Past Symbols of Success

- fame
- being in *Who's Who*
- five-figure salary
- college degree
- splendid house
- executive position
- new car every year
- membership in the club

Present Symbols of Success

- unlisted phone number
- Swiss bank account
- connections with celebrities
- deskless office
- second and third house
- owning a rare foreign car
- being a vice president
- being published
- frequent and unpredictable world travel

Future Symbols of Success

- free time anytime
- recognition as a creative person
- oneness of work and play

- rewarded less by money than by honor and affection
- major societal commitments
- easy laughter, unembarrassed tears
- wide-ranging interests and activities
- philosophical independence
- loving—in touch with self

If some of these status symbols set off your salivary glands, naturally you'll want a career that will allow you to obtain the ones you want. If none of these interest you, maybe you aren't what SRI calls an Achiever; maybe you're an Emulator or a Belonger, maybe even Inner-Directed. For our purposes, the profundity resides in the fact that there are lists, plural. Paul Fussell has authored a book on the American status system entitled *Class.* In it he writes, "The American, almost uniquely, can be puzzled about where in the society he stands. The things that conferred class in the 1930s—white linen golf knickers, chrome cocktail shakers, vests with white piping— are, to put it mildly, unlikely to do so today." The changing symbols of "class" make the status-seeker doubly frustrated and confused, like being in a scavenger hunt where, upon bringing the loot back to the party, the hunter learns a new list has been issued. For the determined scavenger, there is no party, just a continual search. The business of obtaining status is never finished.

This has taken us to the precipice of a great hole in our cultural thinking. Let's look at an analogy suggested by the futility of continual quest for success and its symbols—let's peek into the Grand Canyon and see what we might learn.

The Grand Canyon teaches two lessons. One is that water is stronger than rock, given enough time. The other is that you can climb a mountain in the Grand Canyon, all the way to the summit, and still be in a hole.

The Hole: A Grand Canyon Lesson

The analogy between achievement and climbing a mountain is not only overworked but overrated. Most true achievers demonstrate a genius for going around mountains or flying above them. Yet the climber analogy must not be dismissed so glibly, for it is one of the contemporary beliefs that shape our vision of life; we must treat it seriously. Here is what the "climber" metaphor really says:

1. Climb for the sake of climbing: the old "because it was there" philosophy.

2. The object is "conquest"; in other words, to get to the top alive and in as little time as possible.

3. The rougher the going and the more danger, the better. A "serious" climb requires grim determination.

One can imagine Dickensian industrialists delighting in the above, eager to fill their ranks with those who ask nothing of the mountain but that it "be there," who expect to exhaust themselves at grave tasks, unable to relax for fear of falling, inching up, up, up.

Occasionally a well-trained climber just lets go. I

have already recounted for you my realization that my career mountain was in the Grand Canyon (remember me shouting into an undialed telephone?), and of my letting go. Where did I land? Not just in new dual careers, but amid a new set of heroes and in a fresh *zeitgeist*, a new spirit.

Without a mountain to climb, I sought a career philosophy to replace climbing merely to reach the top. I needed a new self-image. I settled upon *explorer*. A climber points to a pile of rocks and boasts, "I was there," and calls the mountain "conquered." The explorer goes in search of the new and different, looking for a better place to live.

How an explorer infuriates a serious climber! The explorer is constantly stopping to examine stones or to point out formations, wandering into caves, infatuated by the mountain, not the climb; continually drifting from the trail, in no hurry. Could I "conquer" a mountain? Ha! Conquer it? By climbing on it? No, I wanted to fall in love with the mountain, to have *it conquer me!*

When a person ceases mere climbing and finds a mountain to love, the business-before-pleasure dichotomy melts away; no risk of a forty-year climb up a mountain only to discover it was in the Grand Canyon all along.

And when one wanders off the climber's path, one finds a different class of people, all manner of pioneers and frontiersmen. Between here and the last page of this book I will introduce you to some of those I've met. For the most part, these aren't traditional success-book heroes. Few are famous. Only one has been profiled in *People* magazine, none are among the *Forbes* 400 richest people in America.

During the course of writing this book I was often asked to detail my criteria for the achievers I included. Most of those asking the question seemed to want a yardstick, something "scientific." But I cautioned them about the common-denominator trap discussed earlier and about observing the *aftereffects* of accomplishment as opposed to accomplishment itself. To study, say, the philosophies of the *Forbes* 400 in order to draw conclusions about making money can be like standing at the finish line of the Boston Marathon and drawing conclusions about how to be a runner—one might just walk away determined to spend hundreds of hours practicing dropping sweating to the ground. No, I want you to see those in the act of achievement. And I want to introduce you to those who have not just wealth, but wealths, those who are doing something satisfying with their lives, those who are making *more* than money.

Falling in Love with the Mountain

- *Mark Nykanen, investigative reporter, NBC News*: "My life is like the country-western song, 'Gettin' paid for what I'd be doing anyway.' To be good, you have to feel a passion."

- *Harry Wolf, architect*: "When you work at something that doesn't interest you, it drains you, dries you out. When you work at something you love, the work gives you energy, sits you on a spiral of energy."

- *Anne Studabaker, executive editor, Madison Avenue*: "I will not stay in a job situation where

I'm not learning; there is too much going on in life to just earn money."

- *John Ciardi, poet*: "Language had always been to me what I suppose music must be to a composer. It is the quickening thing, the medium that makes possible. Translation: I am a word-freak."

- *Frederick B. Rentschler, president and chief executive officer, Beatrice Foods:* "[My advice] to any young man or woman pursuing a business career: early on make sure you enjoy what it is that you do. Choose a profession that 'turns you on.' "

- *Faye Landey, entrepreneur*: "I feel I have a destination—still don't know what it is. I 'travel' for the 'sake of travel'—love adventure. Perhaps this is my destination."

- *Andreas Brown, owner, Gotham Book Mart*: "My lawyers and accountants think I'm an eccentric. They tell me things like, 'You could put your capital in municipal bonds and make more money, without the headaches.' It makes no sense to them that I find my work interesting and worthwhile."

A romance with one's work is, for me, the preeminent precondition of success. How could I, or you, count a person successful if he or she doesn't find his or her work worthwhile, a turn-on, a source of energy? And what about money? Achievers such as those I've just quoted are well paid—they are bright and hard-working and either at or headed for the top of their professions. But money was never the principal criterion in the choice of a career. *First,* they had a passion; the passion gave them the energy and courage to get out of line, to be different, which in turn gave them a shot at true excellence. That last sentence is so critical to the thesis of this book that I would like to illustrate it as follows:

The Accomplishment Spiral

Renewed passion

Accomplishment

Innovation (self-reliant, out-of-line thinking)

Energy, commitment, courage

Passion

Self-reliance

How different this spiral is from the popular philosophy of success, from self-help books that teach one how to "psych up" (which simply means to search *inside* for energy), to "get motivated" (read, "turn *yourself* on"), and, in general, to flog yourself with philosophy. To true achievers, "getting motivated" is literally a nonsensical notion.

But you won't find "passion" at the top of a column of "positions available" want ads. Where do you find it? It's like looking for love. No, it's not *like* looking for love, it *is* looking for love—it's the search for a romance with work. Most "career counseling" boils down to matching a person's attributes to a job's attributes, rather like a computer dating service. But the effect is that the "career counselor" simply recommends a line to jump into. We want more. We need a deeper understanding. Let's begin with a review of the best available research on job satisfaction.

Rewards

B. F. Skinner once gave this description of bingo players:

> They sit for hours, listening with extraordinary care to numbers being called out and placing counters on numbers with great precision. What would you give, as an industrialist, if your labor force worked that hard and that carefully!

What generates such an attention level? I don't play bingo, but I suppose that most players understand that in the long run they must *lose money*. Certainly they would be financially better off spending those hours working. But money is a great *positive reinforcement*, right? Not always, according to Skinner:

You work and you get paid. But you don't work
on Monday morning for something that is going
to happen on Friday afternoon, when you get
your paycheck. You work on Monday morning
because there is a supervisor who can fire you if
you don't work. You are actually working to
avoid the loss of the standard of living main-
tained by that paycheck.

So when wages are a chief motivator, they are
negative reinforcement. Indeed, lurking in our collective unconscious is the notion that work should *not*
be intrinsically rewarding, not for its own sake. For
instance, psychologist E. L. Deci recruited students
to work on a "puzzle task" during each of three
sessions. During the course of each session, the participants were given free time in which they could
either continue to work on the puzzles, or read current issues of magazines. None of these students
expected to be paid for their efforts, but *some* nonetheless were given a participation fee at the end of
either the first or second of the three sessions. The
effect: Those who had been previously paid for their
efforts showed a decrease in the amount of free time
spent on the problem-solving task. (Time spent on
the puzzle increased slightly for the control cell, the
unpaid group.)

Here we see the role of money in consciously or
unconsciously separating work from play. Most people simply do not expect to enjoy that for which they
get paid, never think to search for a passion, never
begin the spiral toward excellence.

Despite our cultural clichés, it is in reality impossible to separate work from play; the work environ-

ment is slowly, relentlessly impressing itself upon the worker ... water is stronger than rock. Karl Marx's social philosophy was wrong conclusion upon bad assumption, but one of his insights still reverberates in my head: he understood that the man who, say, makes soap, is himself being made; the soap makes the soapmaker. Work affects self-image, and self-image is what a man thinks—and thus makes—of himself. Freud said it this way: "A man with a toothache cannot fall in love." And a man with a toothache of a career can't fall in love with his work.

Good news: There are types of work, even certain types of large organizations, where a romance with work becomes possible. David Berlew put together a paradigm of what he calls "Organization Emotions and Modes of Leadership" that provides a useful description of work environments. Notice that Berlew's "Stage 3" organization is one characterized by satisfaction and excitement, with values that include self-reliance and meaningful work. Notice that such organizations require "charismatic" leadership. To an "explorer" seeking employment, I'd recommend keeping a copy of Berlew's model in my pocket.

The excellence experts, Thomas J. Peters and Robert H. Waterman, Jr., recommend in their book *In Search of Excellence* an essentially "charismatic" (Stage 3) leadership style. (I think it would be fair to summarize *In Search* as an invitation to managers to be less "scientific" and more "excited.") Peters and Waterman studied profitable Fortune 500 companies, whereas Berlew's work was vintage early 1970s—he sought to explain why professionals leave "apparently well-managed organizations" in search of "something more." And not surprisingly, Berlew's

---

ORGANIZATIONAL EMOTIONS
AND MODES OF LEADERSHIP

STAGE 1	STAGE 2	STAGE 3

Emotional Tone:

Anger or			
Resentment	Neutrality	Satisfaction	Excitement

Leadership Mode:

CUSTODIAL	MANAGERIAL	CHARISMATIC

Focal Needs or Values:

Food	Membership	Meaningful work
Shelter	Achievement	Self-reliance
Security	Recognition	Community
Fair treatment		Excellence
Human dignity		Service
		Social Responsibility

Focal Changes or Improvements:

Working conditions	Job enrichment	Common vision
Compensation	Job enlargement	Value-related
Fringe benefits	Job rotation	opportunities and
Equal opportunity	Participative	activities
Decent supervision	management	Supervision that
Grievance procedures	Management by	strengthens
	objectives	subordinates
	Effective supervision	

1970s' "touchy-feely" concerns are almost indistinguishable from Peters's and Waterman's hard-headed profitability ones in *In Search of Excellence*; yesterday's protest organizers are today's innovators.

But how is a lone individual to achieve and maintain what Berlew might call a "Stage 3" life, especially if he or she doesn't want to search inside large organizations? The chapter that follows will assist in the search for such a career; but before we get to that point, we must make our way out of the Grand Canyon.

Water Is Stronger Than Rock: Another Grand Canyon Lesson

It occurred to me that perhaps success and career passion had between them nothing more than what we in research call a "spurious correlation," one of those relationships like that between stock prices and the length of women's skirts—correlation but no causation. It was possible, I told myself, that special achievers are simply those who love a challenge, any challenge; and, if life had cast them in the role of, say, traffic cop, they would be one of those singing, dancing policemen that local news shows profile. In other words, could it be that their careers are simply the result of "positive thinking," that these are people who would have loved any career, been happy anywhere? The answer, and I think this important, is NO.

So what of "water is stronger than rock"? As I mentioned at the outset of this chapter, we—our generation—are positive thinkers. We were raised on Locker Room Wisdom. For instance, on the wall of the locker room where I went to high school was this epigram:

Winners never quit.
Quitters never win.

I suspect it was somewhere in your school too. The sports teams that every day dressed and undressed beneath that banner rarely won a game. But we never thought to question Locker Room Wisdom. We had only one answer—Try Harder!—and were allowed no questions.

Do I sound a bit resentful? Well, I am. Positive thinking is a comfortable religion that tells us that if only we *thought differently* about the world, our problems would melt away. Everything will work out if only you believe it will. Wait. Believe. Overcome. You are stronger than your situation.

All religions are based on hope, but positive thinking is based on nothing else. It even has its own faith healing, asserting that diseases can be overcome with optimism. Any disease, even cancer, is said to be a case of negative thinking. (This makes me wonder why lab rats get cancer so regularly. Do rats have a death wish? Try to club one.)

The truth is this simple: in the long run, an individual is *not* stronger than his or her situation. In the long run, *you are your situation.* To believe differently is to risk spending your life cursing, "I am happy, damn it!" I have picked two short career stories to illustrate my point. These are examples of happy, successful people who could, had they been a trifle more "sensible" as rookies, be sorrowful middle-aged people today.

■ DONALD WELSH, now a publisher, was once a "miserable" lawyer. Mr. Welsh went to law school for his father's sake. Like so many students, he rarely thought about his actual work or the life he would lead—he was preoccupied with getting through school. But having graduated and landed a job, he discovered this: "The work was boring, dull. And *because I felt that way, I wasn't a very good lawyer.*"

Mr. Welsh could have told himself to quit whining and be happy. He could have looked on law school and his first year as a lawyer—four years of his life!—as an investment that would be lost by changing careers. Instead, he asked himself what it was he really wanted. The answer: "I discovered that down deep I had always known what I wanted to do. I started a magazine when I was in the sixth grade and I had been editor of my high school paper: I had always wanted a career in magazines, in magazine publishing."

So he went out and found a position selling advertising space for *Fortune.* No, not his "dream job," not yet, but closer. Then he became advertising director for *Rolling Stone* and was eventually promoted to associate publisher, which led to the position of publisher of *Outside* magazine. In this last job he planned and developed a new magazine, one for kids, entitled *Muppet Magazine.* When *Outside* didn't share his enthusiasm for the project, he bought the rights to it and, as part of a prospering television company, Telepictures, Inc., became the publisher of *Muppet Magazine.* Despite starting along the wrong career path and having to double back, Mr. Welsh had, before the age of forty, his own magazine, the first of several.

Notice what Donald Welsh said about being a lawyer: *he wasn't very good at it because he didn't have a passion for it.* Donald Welsh is a bright and personable man; he could have stayed in law and earned a sizable salary. Maybe with enough positive thinking he could have developed a passion for law.

Maybe not. But he did the wise thing: discovered his passion and followed *it* rather than trying to coax his passions to follow *him*.

■ TAMARA THOMAS's career story has a twist: she didn't find her way out of line, she refused to get into one. After earning a bachelor of arts degree in art history from the University of California at Berkeley, she rejected the only jobs open to her—"a teacher or a lowly museum job"—and went instead to Europe, intending to go to graduate school but ending up staying five years, "working odd jobs."

Ms. Thomas knew she wanted certain things in her career—she did not want to be an artist, but to work with artists and art—but knew of no jobs that fit these requirements. She only knew that she would wait, that she would not compromise her passions.

Then, at a cocktail party in New York, she met a woman who specialized in "putting artists and architects together. For example, if an architect needed a special screen in one of his buildings, he would call this woman." Ms. Thomas became her assistant. Two years later, in 1970, she opened an art consulting business of her own, Fine Arts Services, Inc. Now she purchases artwork for over forty major clients, buying millions of dollars of art a year on their behalf. She was called by *New West* "the West Coast's premier art consultant and one of the most powerful art brokers in the country . . . a Bernard Berenson to corporate America."

I'm sure that friends of Ms. Thomas, before her success, must have thought her stubborn or childish. Surely they slapped their foreheads and cried, "Be realistic. Quit being so picky. Try to think positively."

Ask a large number of people for their opinions and they will, on average, recommend being average. The average person isn't quickened, passionate, energetic, or turned-on, so it is not surprising that achievers tend to be independent thinkers who found their careers, if not by trial and error, by listening to the voice of a passion deep within.

Mr. Welsh and Ms. Thomas have distinguished themselves because they were explorers, not climbers. They had to be critical, to be "negative thinkers," if you will, in order to escape the tyranny of the obvious in order to do something other than to maximize next year's income. In short, they both had to be stubborn enough to be creative. Creativity begins with a pigheaded refusal to accept what's good enough for everybody else. And the fingerprint of passion is upon any endeavor that chooses excitement over income. In conclusion: *A successful career begins not with positive thinking but with passionate thinking.*

One final caution: Please don't leave this chapter determined to find the one-and-only "perfect job." Just as I have made wealth into the plural, wealths, we need to do the same for passion. Most people can answer with one word the question, "What do you do?" I believe this singularity is related to the mountain-climber mentality, to the notion that we should be propelled toward one major career goal; i.e., getting to the top of the mountain. But passions don't have to be singular or linear. I recently asked Jonathan Miller (the physician, author, and producer-director) if he ever wishes he had specialized in just one of his careers. He replied:

> I specialized in *all* my careers. I spend a great deal of time working it up, coming up to the standards of the profession. Specialization is nothing but answerability to a clientele. But I'm also an objector to specialization. It is an attempt to guarantee professionalism when in doubt about the status of an undertaking. The real test of a career is this: is it of interest, does it make a contribution?

The more that interests you, the more likely you are to be interested. The broader a person's passion, the broader the person. It might seem that the more specific the goal, the greater the likelihood of success; but the opposite is true. The narrower the career path, the more easily it is blocked. I asked Dr. Miller, a true Renaissance Man, if he had ever failed at a career. At first he said, "No, I've chosen what I do because I'm good at it"; then he cocked an eyebrow and added, "Yes. I once undertook pathology and gave it up. Detested it." So even a Renaissance Man has the sense to admit a career failure, not to throw good time after bad. That is one glory of refusing to specialize—a career interest can be added or subtracted without major disruption; one is free to emphasize that aspect of a career where the greatest progress is, at that moment, possible. And one is free to let passions evolve and mature.

Enough philosophy! It's time to move on to more practical matters, time to get down to business—

yours. There are five truths I want you to take along:

- Movement is not accomplishment—there are mountains even in the Grand Canyon.
- The dichotomy between work and play is a false one.
- The explorer, not the mountain climber, is the one likely to discover a better place to dwell.
- Accomplishment is a spiral that originates with self-reliance and a passion for work.
- The more wealths one recognizes, the greater the likelihood of being wealthy.

CHAPTER 2

YOUR MAP OF THE FUTURE

---■---

Such gardens are not made
By singing:—"Oh, how beautiful!" and
sitting in the shade.

Rudyard Kipling
"The Glory of the Garden"

Former Secretary of the Treasury William Simon once said, "The nation should have a tax system that looks like someone designed it on purpose." The same could be said for a person's career, and the remainder of this book teaches the art of *purposeful career crafting.* This is not to say that I'll ask you to plan your entire life here, today—who would want a life without change, without surprise? No, I think a career should be written the way many novels are: once you get the right characters and setting, the plot evolves itself. When such a book is closed, even though the author chose not to construct the plot in advance, the result is as if all that transpired was very much thought out, very much on purpose.

Consider the title character in your career story.

Just what sort should he or she be? What should he/she care about? Desire most?

Because I revel in human diversity, I will resist writing your story for you, resist telling you what you *should* desire. Rather, my purpose will be that of a guide, helping you recognize all your choices among all there is to worldly existence—people, possessions, and time.

You Are Your Colleagues

First, in the belief that people are the most important of riches, let's begin by defining the sort of people with whom you want to associate.

Although some of us are unwilling to admit it, the people who surround us profoundly influence us; they pull us the way the planets silently, endlessly tug at one another. You are at this moment in the process of becoming your co-workers. Consider this experiment by psychologists Eliot Aronson and David Mettee:

A group of student volunteers was given a personality test. One-third of the sample was given positive feedback (the conclusion that they were "interesting, mature, deep," etc.), another third was given negative feedback (told they were "immature, shallow," etc.), and the remaining third got no feedback. Next, the students went on to participate in a second, seemingly unrelated experiment, a game of cards. However, the card game was rigged so that the participants could cheat and thereby win "a considerable sum of money, or not cheat, in which case they were sure to lose." The researchers report that "the students who received blows to their self-esteem cheated far more than those who had gotten positive feedback about themselves."

It's been said, "You are not what you think you are; you are not what other people think you are; you are what you think other people think you are." In other words, self-esteem is a vote in which you count the ballots. This doesn't mean you'll like the results: after Dick Tuck lost a race for California assemblyman he told his supporters, "The people have spoken—the bastards." But in your career you needn't let bastards vote; not, that is, if you pick your colleagues well.

Exercise Number 1

Your Closest Colleague

Let's begin by picturing your closest colleague ... *ten years from now.* You may not even know what sort of career you want to be in, but you still can establish one sort of person you want to work with. (You may have many types of people you desire to associate with. That's good. But for now I want you to idealize just one. Or you may plan a solitary career, say, as a painter. In this case, envision a fellow painter, your agent, or the owner of the gallery where your work is shown.)

Consider your closest colleague as the main character in your career story. Just what sort should he or she be? What should he or she care about? Desire most?

To help you get specific, I have put together a list of characteristics as a jumping-off point:

> intelligence
> looks
> athletic ability
> openness/emotionalism
> education
> leadership ability
> religious involvement/attitudes
> political involvement/attitudes
> energy
> work skills/professionalism
> social involvement/attitudes
> creativity
> willingness to change/innovate
> power/influence
> wit
> confidence/assertiveness

Each of the characteristics listed above could have many manifestations. If you want peers who are well-educated, you could define that as "advanced degrees from leading universities," "well-read in the humanities," "graduate of the school of hard knocks," or any one of a dozen definitions. Since it's your future, you get to do any further defining.

If you're still having trouble conjuring up your closest colleague, try looking at an empty chair or a blank wall and imagining that it is ten years in the future and that you are sitting across from him or her. You needn't try to give a face or body to the colleague, but I am asking you to answer for this colleague, "Who are you?" Record a few phrases that help define that person—perhaps it's the position they hold, how they look, how they act, how they feel, what they know, who they know, and so on. Do this ten times—each time adding a new characteristic of the person's personality, appearance, capabilities, or positions.

Exercise Number 2

More Colleagues

If you were able to define your closest colleague, you should now try to envision additional colleagues. These people may be quite different from, or quite similar to, your "closest colleague"—it's up to you—extending the exercise permits as much diversity as you desire.

If you were unable to envision the sort of person you want to be around in your work environment, you are destined to remain blindfolded in your search for fulfillment. The lone exception to this rule is the misanthrope, the person who realizes that he or she simply does not want to be around *any* other people. Others may attempt to shirk this task by simply defining success as "not doing any work." For the latter group, I urge you to reconsider your goal, or at least to consider redefining your definition of "work." I have never met a happy man who did not throw himself into his endeavors.

Exercise Number 3

A Week in the Life

Now, with some notion of your ideal colleagues, let's move on to envisioning a typical week in your life ten years from now, *after you have achieved the success you desire.* Divide the week into various activities, including sleep, work, time with friends, time devoted to hobbies, exercise, recreation, education, reading, and so forth. There are 168 hours in a week. If you take away fifty to sixty hours for time spent in bed, and some hours for eating and bathing, you have a base of convenient size for calculation, roughly 100 hours per week. I'd include at least these activities in divvying up those 100 hours: time at your place or places of work, time with hobbies, friends, in exercise, education, and recreation.

Money and Other Fears

Now that we have dealt with time and people, we turn to places and possessions.

There seems to be a new materialism abroad in the land. Take, for instance, these scenes from two of the most popular movies in recent years.

Risky Business

The setting: A group of adolescents—high-school seniors from an upscale Chicago suburb—are seated around a table in a fast food restaurant, discussing college admissions and possible careers. (Because it is the season for college acceptance letters, the conversation has an underlying urgency.)

The scene begins with one of the students telling the others that a classmate has been accepted to Harvard.

GLEN: Do you know what a Harvard MBA makes, first year? Forty grand.
GIRL: Well, I have a cousin that went into dermatology. First year, over sixty thousand.
BARRY: Just for squeezing zits?
GLEN: You ought to try it, Barry; you've got the experience.
BARRY: Thank you. You're very kind.
JOEL: Hey listen, you guys, I mean doesn't anyone want to accomplish anything or do we just want to make money?
BOY: Make money.
GIRL: Just make money.
BARRY: Yeah.
GLEN: Make a lot of money.
GIRL: How about you, Joel?
JOEL: (*Pause. Looks away*) Serve my fellow mankind.

Joel grins. All others throw french fries at him, saying at once "shit" and "get out of here."

Okay, so maybe we can't expect deep thinking about careers from high-school seniors. (Although this is the time when most career decisions are made, many irrevocably so.) But we find like attitudes in *The Big Chill*, a movie that was taken to the breast of the Baby Boom generation.

The Big Chill

The setting: A weekend-long reunion of former
college pals has resulted from the suicide of one
member of the old clique. Two of the friends,
Harold and Sam, now in their middle thirties,
are catching up on each other's accomplishments
as they make up a spare bed in Harold's country manor home. They are nouveaux riches—
Harold owns a chain of sporting shoe shops,
ironically called "The Running Dog" (remember Marx and the "running dogs of capitalism"?),
while Sam is the lead actor on a television series.

SAM: How many [stores] does that make now?
HAROLD: That's twenty-seven and twenty-eight.
SAM: (*Whistles*) Better watch out, some big mon-
ster is gonna buy ya.
HAROLD: We've had offers.
SAM: Who would've thought we'd both make
so much bread? Two revolutionaries.
HAROLD: Yeah. (*Ironically*) Good thing it's not
important to us.
SAM: Right. Fuck 'em if they can't take a joke.

Willem de Kooning said, "The trouble with being
poor is that it takes up all your time." And anyone
preoccupied with getting richer is poor. The solutions are three: (1) lead an ascetic life and thereby
keep monetary requirements to a minimum; (2) find
something you enjoy doing for which you can re-
ceive a decent income; (3) do something you hate
but which is lucrative until you have accumulated
enough money to leave the philistine enterprise for a
more satisfying one.

48

Most people I have met have chosen the third option. *It simply does not work.* You may remember Parkinson's Law: "Work expands to fill the time allotted to it." There is a related dictum, Parkinson's Second Law, which says: "Expenses rise to equal income." And I'd propose one more, let's call it Hunt's Law: "No matter how large your income, poverty tends to be less than three months away."

I chose the appellation "Hunt's Law" after the family of H. L. Hunt, partly in honor of the sons, the ones who practically lost their monogrammed shirts in the 1980 silver tumble, but more so after the sister, Caroline Hunt Schoellkopf, who has, according to *Forbes*, a minimum net worth of $1.3 billion but who told the magazine, "All my life I thought I'd wind up penniless."

Most people, even those with vast incomes, cannot countenance one month without the accustomed level of income, much less three. Sure, some people are able to save money and others aren't, but saving is a form of spending. People who put money into savings either are accumulating money toward some future purchase or else they save for saving's sake, to acquire the sense of security it provides. Once money has been saved, to begin using it is to begin consuming security for the future—how frightening, how psychologically impoverishing! You must not expect that you can acquire so much wealth that losing a bit of it won't hurt. Think of Caroline Hunt Schoellkopf worrying about winding up penniless.

Furthermore, the less money you require, the more career options you have. Instead of asking you how much money you'd like to have (the answer is obvious), I'd like you to think about what possessions you actually need to consider yourself fulfilled.

Exercise Number 4

Possessions Inventory

Make a list of the possessions you will require to live *comfortably*. (Assume that you have a thoroughly rewarding career and some engaging noncareer activities.) I'd include in the list:

- *Living space* (number of rooms required, amount of land, quality or fashionableness of the architecture)
- *Transportation* (number and quality of autos, accessibility of other forms of transportation)
- *Wardrobe* (extent and quality of apparel)
- *Entertainment* (type and frequency of activities)
- *Whatever other possessions* you need for physical or psychic comfort, including your special requirements that are of great personal importance (for example, a fishing boat or a library)

Some people balk when asked to contemplate a list of possessions necessary for a comfortable life. They simply say they want the finest of possessions and an unlimited number of them, quoting Oscar Wilde, "My tastes are very simple: I require only the finest."

I do not dismiss vanity and competitiveness as unimportant or even undesirable; however, for the intelligent and sensitive person, there are usually better ways to satisfy those natural acquisitive instincts. No, I'm not going to ask you to think of the poor or of starving children, but I will invite you to observe those who place their pride in their knowledge of their artistic development or their experiences. Then go back and look again at the status symbols of the future presented in Chapter 1 (pages 20–21), and see anew that material wealth as *the* definition of wealth is obsolete.

Indeed, I have observed how often achievers pass up status symbols, even those they could readily afford. The magazine *M* did a feature called "Men and Their Cars" (May 1984) and reported the following:

Man	*Car*
Carter Brown Director, National Gallery	1980 Honda Civic
Sydney Gruson Vice Chairman, N.Y. Times Co.	1971 Jaguar, 1982 Oldsmobile
Malcolm Forbes Editor, *Forbes*	Lamborghini, more than 20 motorcycles
Jim Baker President Reagan's Chief of Staff	1977 Chevrolet Suburban
Clark Clifford Former Secretary of Defense	1980s Chrysler
William F. Buckley, Jr.	1970s Cadillac limousine, 2 Volvos

Conclusions? Since I know that Buckley has a desk set up in his limo so that he can get in extra hours of work each week (time that is of sufficient value to more than pay the expense of the limo), it looks as if *practicality* is the most important criterion, doesn't it?

(Mr. Forbes seems to be the lone exception.) As long as we're doing exercises, let me ask this: Why is practicality preeminent? My answer is that these men are, we must assume, passionate about their careers; they get their ego gratification somewhere other than the streets.

Exercise Number 5

Geography

In a conversation with Alejandro Menendez, one of the world's most accomplished ballet dancers, a man whose work has taken him all over the world, I fell into a familiar debate: the best city in which to live. I cursed the weather of one city, I can't remember which one, but I recall him bringing me up short with this comment: "I wouldn't halt my career for the sake of a suntan."

Not all geographical decisions are so apparent. Just as the people who surround you are shaping your personality, so does your place of residence pinch and mold your psyche like an unseen potter. What location would best suit your purpose? Having previously defined your ideal colleagues, allocated your time, and specified your possessions, you may find that you have, in so doing, delineated your geographical possibilities. But even within a country and city, you still have choices.

Ten years out, when you're a success, what or whom must you be near? The office? Church? Relatives? Arts? (Here's a simple calculation that many of my acquaintances forget: If you could live ten minutes away from work instead of forty minutes, that's

250 hours a year of driving time saved, or over six forty-hour weeks every year.)

And what do you want from a neighborhood? Stimulation? Friendship? Contacts? Walden Pond peace and solitude?

Exercise Number 6

The Map

I've heard it said that people tend to judge a person by his goals, rather than by the actual achievement of those goals. I think this is the way you should judge yourself. A friend of mine, Lucy O'Brien— one of the pioneer newspaperwomen in Florida, now an entrepreneur—put it this way: "The most important question a person ever asks is, 'If I die today, what will my life have stood for?' " If you have goals, you'll always be able to answer that question.

And yet I meet many people whose goals are but admirable dreams, for they have let themselves be put into situations that afford no possibility of the achievement they see for themselves. They seem not to notice; they talk about faith in themselves and their futures; they work and they worry, assuming that somehow some success god will see how fast and straight they run and pluck them up into achiever's heaven. You've heard them: "Just do your job as well as you can do it and the future will take care of itself." Do they really believe that God has become the Great Career Planner and is at this very moment plotting their job promotion? They are like the captain of a sailing ship who proudly trusts the winds to take him to his destination.

What I'd suggest to the captain of your ship is a check of the stars. Telescope down your current route and see where you're going. All that we have done in this chapter was in preparation for the exercise that follows. Now that you have begun to consider the type of people you want to associate with, the type of place in which you want to live, and how you want to live, it is time to evaluate your current circumstances, to see whether you are heading there.

Life slaps us slowly with the lesson that our environment tends to be stronger than we are. The path you are now traveling is straighter than you care to think and you can see farther than you might guess. I want you to write out (or tape-record) what your life will be like in ten years if you pursue the career you are in, or the career you are contemplating entering. Be optimistic—assume you will advance faster than an ordinary bright young man or woman in your field. What we are seeking is not a date of arrival, but how you will like it when you get there.

The year is 19____. (Ten years from today.) You are just arriving at work. Describe what time it is, what you are wearing, and what your office or other work area looks like.

Describe your boss, if you have one. (How do you feel about him or her? Describe your relationship.)

Describe your peers and others you associate with during the course of a day. (How do you relate to them? How do you feel about them?)

Describe the work you are doing. (Is it interesting, rewarding? If you did it for the rest of your life, would you be satisfied?)

You are now leaving work to head to your house. How do you feel about the day you have just spent?

You arrive home. What time is it? What do you find there?

There it is—your future. Want it?

Rosa Parks, the woman who began the Montgomery bus boycott by refusing to yield her seat to a white man (it was, you'll recall, the Montgomery bus boycott that brought Martin Luther King, Jr., to national attention), was asked how she felt walking to work rather than riding the bus. She said, "My feet is tired, but my soul is rested." That, I submit, is how you should feel about your career. Sure, if you care, you'll work hard, your brain or your feet or your back will ache, but oh, your soul will be rested.

If thinking about your future along the same career path puts your soul at ease, congratulations. It is as profound a pleasure as any on earth to have a sense of purpose, a destiny. If, however, a glimpse of your future did not assuage your spirit, you face the greatest challenge of your life—determining a new self, giving birth to yourself. I urge you not to hurry this decision, but to take as many weeks or months as you need. I urge you to try out potential careers using the "map of the future" technique. Take a picture of your future self and then compare it to all that has gone before in this chapter—your image of the ideal colleagues, the ideal use of time, and the requisite possessions and geography. You may have more than one career that meets your criteria of success, and may even be able to work on more than one career simultaneously.

I'd also rely upon mapping to assist you in career decisions. I opened this chapter by saying that a career should be authored like a good novel—if you know the characters well enough, the plot falls into place. The map of the future is simply a way of envisioning the plot and thereby testing whether or not it fits the characters. For example, say you are a young banker with a job offer from a competing bank—to be a bond trader at another two grand a year and with an extra half-hour a day for lunch. Can't pass that up, right? First, I'd take a longer view—consult the map. If our young banker knows he is really suited to being an entrepreneur, the new job might just be a career demotion, one that would prevent him from learning more about financial management of small companies, and one that would diminish his experience among entrepreneurs.

Before we leave this section, let me tell two true success stories. These are stories *People* magazine would scoff at, I suppose, but they are ones that, if I do not miss my guess, will mean much more to the readers of this book than would another account of, oh, Mary Kay and her pink bathtub. In these stories we meet two young professionals who, with procedures similar to those I have just proposed, found their passions and began a romance with work. To do so, each had to glimpse what awaited him along the route of the career bus he was riding, jump off, and run the other direction until his feet were weary and his . . . well, you know the rest.

■ BOB JOHNSON, MBA in hand, began the "upward march" that was to end in MBA heaven (a place about eighty stories high, with oak paneling and an electric shoe buffer in the men's room). He started by becoming a product manager for Armour-Dial, the consumer products division of Armour and Company. (He was in line.)

But after a few years he had a "falling out" with the director of marketing and was shunted off into that dreaded corporate purgatory, a staff position, training rookie product managers and working on computer models. (Out of line.)

This started him on a search for a new job, a new line. But his heart wasn't, quite literally, up to it. He was hospitalized with pericarditis, an infection of the sac around the heart. Nine days in the hospital gave Bob Johnson something product managers don't often get: time to reflect. He reevaluated his career and found:

1. He preferred purgatory to heaven. Ever since he had been given the "undesirable" assignment of training young employees and doing marketing modeling, his job had become more satisfying, not less. He was actually enjoying himself. Could his boss make the same statement? The president? Hard to tell. Bob Johnson could move to a new company, start over and spend twenty years clawing his way to the uncertain joy of the presidency, or keep on enjoying himself.

2. But how long would he remain satisfied in his current position? He was ambitious; he just couldn't be content to work forever in a corporate dressing room, tailoring gray-flannel solutions for others to wear to their inaugurations.

Rubbing these two sticks together, he set his passions on fire . . . a professor! A professor could work with young people and with esoteric models and still be ambitious and innovative.

In a matter of days he had arranged to take the entrance exams for work on a doctorate. Stanford wanted him. Then his course work was finished and the Amos Tuck School at Dartmouth College wanted him. Now academic journals want his articles and corporations want his consultation. Now he picks the problems he solves. Now he is passionate about his career.

■ BARD WRISLEY's early career days were vintage early 1970s: he graduated from college with a degree in political science, traveled to Europe, came home and took a temporary job driving a truck because he "wasn't ready to put on a tie." Finally he began job interviews: "banks, government—the standard list." No takers. "Perhaps," he now conjectures, "if I had gone ahead and shaved my beard, I would today be a loan officer," and he gives a great shudder.

He eventually took a job in his family's food brokerage business. Although the job was often dull, it had rewards—everyone was friendly, he was helping the company grow, and his future was clear. It was the last of these "rewards" that troubled him. He explains:

> If I had been working somewhere else, a large corporation, maybe a bank, I probably would have gotten caught up in climbing the ladder, being competitive, never knowing where I'd be next year. But, since it was a family business,

the ladder was short. It wasn't hard to see my future. Twenty years to move across the desk, to have a job not very different from my own. Where was the excitement?

These visions of his future came after Mr. Wrisley had been in his job about a year. They made him despondent; he had developed friendships and he wanted to be what his co-workers wanted him to be—one of them. But, haunted by the picture of his future, he could not be patient for a success he did not want. Like a man lost in a blizzard, he wanted very badly just to lie down, to relax, to wait. But he forced himself to walk on only because he realized what lying down meant.

He began to analyze careers. He recalled for me his earliest evaluations:

At first I just ran jobs through my head. I started with a primitive system to qualify possible careers. At first I had four pieces of data about myself:

1. I like to work hard, so I know I'll spend three-quarters of my time working; therefore, I'd better have some fun doing it. And there is nothing more fun than success.

2. I want to work with people, but I want to treat them as equals and have them treat me the same way.

3. I didn't want to wait twenty years to have a creative outlet, to have my suggestions taken

seriously. In a large corporation, who's going to listen to a young upstart?

4. My motto is "Question Authority."

That doesn't sound like much, but it was a start. With just those four pieces of data, I could eliminate some careers, but not many. I thought about being a plumber or a lawyer ... everything. So I knew I needed to know more about myself. I started to add income requirements. I added a requirement about being able to take time off. I wanted to live in a major city. I wanted to have an office I could be proud of. I wanted to work around bright, diverse people. I wanted big things and small. But those requirements did not eliminate as many careers as you might think. What I needed was a feeling for what each job would do to my head. This is the hard part to explain. I wanted pressure, but not ulcers, for example. I wanted to work hard, but by my own schedule. I wanted to be forced to think but not to worry. I realized that I could evaluate these things only by getting to know what some possible careers were really like in an everyday sense.

What Bard Wrisley had realized was that a choice of a career was a choice of *the type of man he would become*; he wanted a career that would reward him for being the kind of man he wanted to be. This demanded he take a realistic look at himself and at careers, that he know more about a job than its salary, more even than its "path." He describes how he went about it.

I started to meet new people. I would get together with people in other careers and pick
their brains, learning about what people successful in that job were like.

Soon he had found the right career—photography.

I talked to photographers and got job offers,
sort of: they wanted me to be an apprentice, for
free. But I needed money to live. So I took a
job at a friend's auto-repair shop, with the agree-
ment that I could have time off whenever I
needed it, and I started my own business.
Through a friend at a film company I started
getting some assignments. These didn't pay well,
but they were experience. It took two and a half
years until I was a full-time photographer. Then
I decided that it really was going to happen,
that I really was a photographer and that's exactly what I wanted to be.

And Bard Wrisley keeps discovering. He is considered to be Atlanta's premier commercial photographer. He is working on two books and developing a
new specialty, photographing artists. He knows how
to persevere as well as how to be impatient. He
remains open to adventure.

So we are back where we began: questioning authority, stepping out of line, exploring. If I have
done my job well, the preceding chapters are a guidebook to finding romance with work. But we must not
be content to stop at that, to simply find the best of
all possible career lines and hop into one. No, if a

career is to ride upon what I earlier called "The Accomplishment Spiral," the spirit of self-reliance must prevail. Having found the right career or careers, the creative question changes from, "Is there a better situation?" to, "Is there a better way?"

PART

TWO

Purposeful
Career Crafting

Most people are other people. Their thoughts
are someone else's opinions, their life a mim-
icry, their passions quotations.

OSCAR WILDE

WE AMERICANS ARE THE SONS AND DAUGHTERS OF FRON-
tiersmen and pioneers. Our forefathers thumbed their
noses at every polite society of the past three centu-
ries. We are descendants of black sheep. Perhaps
that is why even now a reverence for the loner—the
cowboy, the inventor, the detective—echoes in our
collective unconscious, and perhaps that is why we
so willingly embrace change. You may remember a
book called *Future Shock*, which appeared during our
brief doomsday period in the seventies, opining that
change was becoming too rapid for us to absorb. Ha!
Afraid of better transportation, medicine, communications? There is no job a robot can do that you or I
would want. No, we remain a people hooked on
innovation. During the 1984 Presidential primaries
Gary Hart almost got himself nominated by promising "new ideas." Alas, whether or not he truly had
them became a matter for debate. For the sake of the
country, I wish Gary Hart and every other senator
would join us for the next two chapters; we are
going to learn to generate cartfuls of innovative ideas,
the sort of creativity that allows a person to be not
only different, but better.

CHAPTER 3

THE EXPLORER

—————————■—————————

Two boys arrived yesterday with a pebble they said was the head of a dog until I pointed out that it was really a typewriter.

Picasso

Let us travel to the very heart of creativity. And let's begin by analyzing the greatest idea of all time, the wheel. Historians disagree as to where and when the wheel was invented, but I know *how* it was invented. It had to be something like this . . . .

The scene: Thousands of years before Christ. A wooded area near the Mediterranean Sea. A local ruler is having a wall built. Two men, Lerkus and Lucilius, have been hired to load stones in sacks and lug them on their backs to the site of the wall.

LERKUS: These stones are most heavy! My back!
LUCILIUS: I know. I too am weary. And I promised Aroma I would return to her tent as

soon as the sun climbs down from the trees. The wench! She is insatiable.

LERKUS: (*Smiling fondly.*) I know.

LUCILIUS: (*Much annoyed.*) How am I to take that? Cad!

The two men commence bickering. Lucilius finally drops his bag of stones, reaches into it, and hurls one at Lerkus. Lerkus hops nimbly out of the stone's path by jumping on top of a log. But when Lerkus lands, the log begins to roll down the slope on which it was resting.

Still holding his sack, the workman dances upon it as it rolls. He finally topples off near the bottom of the hill. Lucilius rushes to see if his friend is injured.

LERKUS: Hurt? I never felt better. I have carried my stones downhill without moving. If only stones had legs!

That night Lerkus diverts himself by trying to tie stick legs on a rock and making it ride a log. Lerkus eventually notices that by sticking one of the "legs" into the hollow end of a round slice of log, he can hold the stone and make the log slice turn. He decides to make the stone into an "ox," and gives it four stick legs and four "hooves" made of slices of logs. Soon the men are selling these primitive carts.

Upon each of the four slices of log on every cart they mark their initials; hence the slices become known as "Ls." Lerkus and Lucilius sell two sizes—"Giant Ls," nearly as tall as a man, and "Wee Ls," about a foot high. Wee Ls catch on.

THE EXPLORER

Forget the pun, but not the lesson. What did it take to make the greatest invention of all time? A stick, a round slice of log with a hole in the middle and, most important, a desire to make stones walk. The last of these is a yearning to be different, to remake the world. Creativity is the opposite of contentment. Creativity is a mind out of line. In any endeavor, the excitement begins when someone says, "Let's do something different." Remember: Different is not always better, but better is always different.

Creativity starts with a *decision* to be creative. Let us think together about a fictitious, general example.

Imagine for a moment that you are the manager of a camera store, and you have just learned that your great-aunt has died and left you sufficient cash to open your own shop. How will you go about it? I'm not talking here about all those little practicalities that you'll find in volumes entitled something like *100 Tips for Opening Your Own Business*. I'm talking about your strategy for building a reputation, a following.

If you are an average, ambitious, hard-working, neophyte businessperson, you will analyze all the camera stores in your city, identify the most successful, and adopt their principles of success as your own. How sound this procedure seems, this simple process of emulation. It *is* logical; it's common sense, the logic of commonness. Think for a moment what this emulation strategy really suggests:

- You choose to copy. Therefore, by definition, there are other stores already doing what you will be doing . . . but they have more experience.

- Your criterion for choosing the stores you'd emulate was their success. But their very success means they have money and influence, large staffs, a wide choice of merchandise.
- Not only does the emulation strategy put you in direct competition with the best, but you won't be able to offer prospective customers anything new.
- The upshot: you start out behind, you stay behind.

There is an advertising axiom that an effective ad combines *association* and *differentiation*. Put another way: tell 'em what it's like, tell 'em how it's different. Marketers call a product that has no differences, one that is nothing but a clone of a previous success, a "me too" brand. The seller moves such a product by investing hefty sums on "image" advertisements, on those ads that try to convince customers that the imitation isn't one. This is an expensive approach to introducing a product, and a risky one as well, for it hinges upon a fundamental lie. But it's *easy*, and it *seems* far safer and more logical than it actually is, so "me toos" continue to flood the market.

Our neophyte shopkeeper can't afford image advertising. He can only succeed by being better. Thus he must start being different. That's when the excitement begins, when someone says, let's do something different. I want to illustrate my assertion with three brief cases. They represent three diverse careers that share one essential common denominator— the will to be unique. Notice in each the *conscious decision* to be unique.

THE EXPLORER

■ IF YOU HAD $1,200, ten years of theatrical experience, and an urge to start your own theater, how would you start? Not through emulation. How about the opposite of emulation?

Listen to the words of Gene Feist, the man who built one of the nation's most successful theaters, the Roundabout, as he describes how it came into existence:

> I don't know how many theaters there were when we started, but there are about 300 professional companies in New York City today. *I knew that if we wanted to attract any attention we had to be distinctive.*
>
> At the time we began, everyone was doing new plays, so we decided to do classics, particularly the nineteenth-century plays.

The Roundabout Theater was born with the will to be different, and that has remained its distinguishing characteristic. Every new production must be subjected to Gene Feist's relentless desire to be better than perfect—classics might be reset in more modern eras, and the staging and the types of actors reinvented with each play. In short, Gene Feist does classics, but with other-than-the-classic presentations, a type of double reversal. Such explorations attract reviewers. An opening at the Roundabout often draws as many as sixty reviews. This coverage, in turn, attracts "name" performers. And all of this attracts an audience—one-quarter of a million people a year, including one of the largest subscriber bases in the country.

TAKING CHANCES

■ NEXT, LET'S ASSUME that you are a musician who has set for yourself the goal of becoming a touring concert performer. How are you going to achieve that goal? Practice, endless practice? Of course. You must perfect your technique. But beyond that, what will your stratagem be? You must study and labor until you can hit every note, until you can play any piece of music exactly as it was written, every note perfect, right? No. Not according to Barry Tuckwell, the world's preeminent horn player:

> The difference between being mediocre and first-class is artistic vision. A note-perfect performance is *not* a perfect performance. The excellent performer takes enormous risks, going beyond his technical capabilities. To play for safety is to ensure a boring performance.

To those who do not understand musical genius, it would seem that music is one endeavor in which imitation is not only desirable but necessary. The composer sets down the music with great care; the musician must simply follow orders. And that is what technically competent musicians do. But a great musician is more than competent. Mr. Tuckwell has studied his flaws in order to perfect his craft, but that is not what makes him outstanding. Indeed, speaking of the technical side of performing, Mr. Tuckwell made this startling statement: "I am not very skillful with my hands." The world's greatest horn player is not very skillful with his hands? Then what makes him great?

No two performances are quite the same. I experiment. To take a simplistic example, I may stretch a phrase or get softer on a given note. I don't need to experiment, the listeners may not quite be aware of it, but it will add color to the performance.

Even with so precise a "map" as a musician has, the great musician is still an explorer.

■ SO WE HAVE EVIDENCE that those involved in the arts *consciously work at being different.* They hold in their minds the typical, the "average," then they experiment with deviations from it. But does such systematic deviation apply in less artistic pursuits? Does it apply to, say, running a sales department?

Chris Roman, who by age twenty-nine was vice-president and director of marketing for a New York television station, said this:

I think of my job as asking the question, Is there a better way? I'm never content with obvious solutions or easy answers. You can always come back to those. When I die the last thing I want people to say about me is that I was predictable. So I keep asking: Are we doing it right? Does it make sense? What are we forgetting? There was a time when all we talked about were problems; now we spend our time talking about solutions.

Those are the words of an explorer. The creative mind is not eager to embrace the easy and obvious, but wants something more, something unique. The ordinary mind is delighted when a problem can be solved readily; Mr. Roman, on the other hand, considers such answers a compromise, something you can always go back to.

There is a great consistency in these stories of discovery, innovation, excellence. The mind of the achiever is full of What-Ifs. By nature a malcontent, the achiever sees all there is and more. Just as Barry Tuckwell asked himself, "What if I played that note more softly?" so Chris Roman asks himself, "Is there a better way?"

Contrarian Creativity

There is a money management strategy known as "contrarian investing." Its essence is to consciously move against money fashions, hoping thereby to heed the first law of successful investing: Buy low, sell high. "Contrarian" also describes at least one aspect of the restless achiever, who, consciously or not, seeks uniqueness, and in so doing, is as interested in *anti*-fashion as most people are in fashion. Often, the simple reversal of convention is all that is necessary to set off sparks of invention.

Don Young, a latter-day Horatio Alger who began his working life as a janitor but who now holds over one hundred patents and was recently named Man of the Year by the American Chemical Society, says his motto is, "If an authority said it, I consider it a challenge." Here's one example of Young's contrarian creativity in action:

We were trying to supply a cheap source of phosphate suitable for agriculture. The old method was to go to the phosphate piles—phosphate contaminated with impurities—and by one method or another remove the impurities. This was an expensive process. All the old attempts to improve the process were new ways to remove the impurities. So I decided that since removing them was causing so many problems, maybe I could find a way to make it possible *not* to remove them. We found a way to surround the impurities and stabilize them, rather like antibodies engulfing germs.

That's contrarian logic. What's the best way to get rid of impurities? Leave 'em in. Here's one more illustration: What's the best way for a journalist to break a news story? See where all the other reporters go and then go somewhere else.

■ FOLLOWING THE FIRE at the MGM Grand Hotel in Las Vegas, Chicago-based Mark Nykanen was one of hundreds of reporters sent to that city in search of news. Many others had a head start on the story, and many knew more about Las Vegas or knew more about fires. How was it then that Nykanen was *the first* to break the story of hotel building-code violations that resulted in the tragedy?

Flying into Las Vegas, I reminded myself that reporters run in packs. Everyone would be chasing the Fire Chief. So I decided right then to forget the Chief and make a list of other possible sources. One of them was Building and Zoning.

Mr. Nykanen found a building inspector who had identified a number of significant violations. He assembled his film crew, "dragged the poor man into a side street," and got his story, one that not only reported the news but made the news.

Even before his feet hit the hot Vegas pavement, Nykanen had made his choice to be contrary. If he had joined the hundreds of reporters loitering outside the office of the Fire Chief, the best he could have hoped for was mediocrity, being one of hundreds sending out the same story. It was only when he consciously decided where he *wasn't* going to get a breakthrough that he gave himself the chance of getting one. And that attitude helps explain why Mark Nykanen, only in his early thirties, is being compared to Mike Wallace. His investigative journalism has already put three Emmys on his mantle, with many to follow, I am certain, for Nykanen is not only intelligent and hard-working, he won't stand in lines.

Systematic Creativity

Achievement begins when someone says, "What if?" But the "what if" question is, of course, incomplete; it begs for completion: "What if we tried _____?" We know that explorers are willing to explore, but *how did they know where to go?*

The preceding cases make plain the individualism of the achievers and how a contrary nature often suffices to suggest alternatives. But as powerful as this "opposites" approach is, it is limited; it is a black-and-white approach that overlooks many colorful solutions. From where do such solutions come?

To answer that question we must first understand the nature of creativity.

Let's begin with an opposite and ask ourselves, why *aren't* people creative? The maturation process consists of learning to conform; that is, *learning to imitate*. For most of us, our creativity reached its peak when we were age five or ten. (Remember when a stick and a tin can could become a hundred games?) But that innate creativity is eventually shamed into hiding. A child is taught that the intellectual, rational, reasoning part of his nature should predominate. Be reasonable. Think it through.

A thoughtful person knows that there is a fundamental duality to human thinking; Nietzsche, for one, named the reasoning side Apollonian, the transcendent side Dionysian. But only recently have we realized that the duality is not just metaphorical; the human brain is actually organized so that the verbal and symbolic functions are typically centered in the left side of the brain, while spatial and intuitive abilities are located in the right. Traditional education is all "left hemisphere," aiding that chatty and demanding left half in its domination of the "uneducated" right half. Meditation and drugs can liberate the right hemisphere; so can creativity exercises. One such exercise (found in Betty Edwards's *Drawing on the Right Side of the Brain*) is to copy, free-hand, an upside-down Picasso sketch. Such an inverted drawing tricks the logical side of the brain.

Failing to impose its normal symbolic sense upon the seemingly nonsensical drawing, the reasoning side of the brain defaults to the creative side. The result is that even those who claim to have no artistic ability can produce a sketch that can be said to demonstrate talent.

What is unfortunate about this left-brain, right-brain talk is that it unintentionally promulgates the notion that creativity is mysterious and alien.

Creativity is not mysterious, dangerous stuff reserved for suicidal poets. *All creativity is simply some recombination of what already exists. And all that inhibits us from seeing new combinations is our training in being logical.*

Let me return to the wheel: It was, like all inventions, the result of either an accidental or intentional recombination. Recall that to have made the greatest invention of all time all you needed was a stick, a round slice of log with a hole in the middle and, most important, a desire to make stones walk. The last of these, the will to discover, is nothing but a *yearning for recombination.* Stones and legs are familiar objects that have yet to be brought together, to be combined. Likewise, wheels-and-axle are merely one combination of something as familiar as logs-and-branches.

Engineers are often given assignments that demand invention. It is not surprising that they, in the most pragmatic of careers, have devised many systematic approaches to creativity. These approaches usually involve little more than a procedure for identifying elements and forcing new combinations of those elements. Take this example from *The Universal Trav-*

eler, a book on creativity written by two designers, Don Koberg and Jim Bagnall:

Here is a foolproof idea-invention-finding scheme:

1. List the attributes of the situation.

2. Below each attribute, place as many alternatives as you can think of. (Use Brainstorming.)

3. When completed, make many random runs across the lists of alternates, picking up a different one from each column and assembling the combinations into entirely new forms of your original subject.

After all, inventions are merely new ways of combining old bits and pieces.

EXAMPLE: Subject: Improve a ball-point pen.

Attributes:	FORM	MATERIAL	CAP DETAIL	INK CARTRIDGE
	Cylindrical	Plastic	Separate cap	Steel cartridge
	Faceted	Metal	Attached cap	Plastic cartridge
	Square	Paper	No cap	Permanent
	Beaded	Wood	Retracts	Paper cartridge
	Sculptured	Glass	Cleaning cap	Cartridge made of ink

INVENTION: A cube pen; one corner writes leaving six faces for ads, calendars, photos, etc.

Another example of forcing new combinations is a computerized procedure for naming new products. Every word with some connection to a product category is fed into a computer. For example, if you wanted to name a new fabric softener, you would list all the "touch" words—like silky, velvety, satiny, and feathery—plus all the "convenience" or "safety" words, or whatever other types of words are or could be relevant to the product. The computer simply electronically pastes together such words, plus all combinations of the syllables that compose the words. The person in charge of product names then reads through a printout consisting of thousands of combinations of syllables and words (things like "silksafe") and circles all those that are pleasing. He or she can thus present the client with a hundred or more alternative names and thereby be considered exceptionally creative.

Do not let these homely little projects—a cube pen and the name of a fabric softener—lead you into a belief that this recombinations approach is a poor relation to "true" creativity. Notice how Gore Vidal describes writing:

> Then there is this business of surprise. I never know what is coming next. The phrase that sounds in the head changes when it appears on the page. Then I start probing it with a pen, finding new meanings. Sometimes I burst out laughing at what is happening as I twist and turn sentences. Strange business all in all. One never gets to the end of it.

That "twisting and turning a phrase" is a series of

experimental recombinations. And think of Picasso's most innovative paintings: what is Cubism but a recombination of the elements of a painting? Picasso's work, perhaps more than that of any other artist, is evidence of the power of recombination.

Given that creativity is a recombination, there is still the task of generating ideas to place in combinations. Have we at last arrived at the point where I advise you to lock yourself in a closet, or in a mountain cabin, and wait for inspiration? Quite the opposite. When Sherlock Holmes was stumped, he would go to an art museum. Why? Sure, it would take him away from the ordinary distractions of the office, but that wasn't his reason—he could have escaped distraction by sticking his head in a drawer. No, what the museum offered was *thousands of new distractions*, every painting a different subject, a different angle. It was full of diverse bits of genius, all candidates for Holmes's subconscious recombination with the problem at hand.

But let us not wait upon the subconscious; let us put the whole process right on top of the mental table. Let us visit two places known for innovation and learn something of the mechanics of invention. I want to prove to you that creativity is not some gift a niggardly angel parcels out at birth, but the result of a conscious process. What I want you to observe is that creativity can be systematic, as opposed to mysterious. There are many systems, but they all accomplish the one task of creativity, bringing together new combinations. In the following chapter I will teach you to use one such procedure, which you will then be able to apply to your work and career goals. In preparation, I would like to show you the recombination process in context. And why not look to the best? ... To Procter and Gamble, the world's leading consumer products company, and to Johnson and Burgee, the nation's leading architectural firm.

■ PROCTER AND GAMBLE is the maker of Tide, Ivory, Sure, Charmin, Downy and dozens of other bestselling household products. How do they do it? Here are the words of Jim Bangel, an internal consultant at P & G, an "idea man" who helps develop the company's new products:

> I go out and find anything in the world remotely related to the project at hand. For instance, if we want to make a product more convenient, I study every success and failure of product convenience for every product in the world.

So if Jim Bangel wanted to make a better pot scrubber, say, he might naturally *begin* by studying every pot scrubber made, establishing a set of norms, defining what he must be better than. But that would be background; he would not expect his ideas to start there, staring at pot scrubbers. The excitement would begin when he began to study ... maybe cigarette lighters, rifles, or beer cans—any invention that might provide elements that he could bring into combination with a pot scrubber.

And when Mr. Bangel collects information on "every success and failure in the world," he isn't merely looking for something to imitate. If he were aiming to imitate, he would be like, as he put it, "those who attempted to fly by putting on wings and flapping their arms." Instead, he is seeking to understand convenience, to define all its functions, to test each of those functions against his product, and to see if any offer a meaningful improvement. Let me illustrate the point by having a go at my pot scrubber example—let me try to bring in a convenience attribute borrowed from a cigarette lighter, rifle, or beer can. If I were to be foolishly literal, I would say, "Pot scrubber + can convenience = a frying pan with a pop-top." Dumb. Like putting on wings. But if I thought about the *convenience* the pop-top represents, I would say, "The opener is *right there*, attached to the can, not off in a drawer somewhere." So I would start to think about how a pot scrubber could be gotten out of the drawer and closer to the task. I might realize that if I could make a pot scrubber handsome, it could be kept out, atop the back of the sink. Maybe it would have a case to store it in. Or maybe it could have some sort of magnet to hold it to the sink when not in use.

I could keep going using the beer can as a model, but then I have a world of ideas to explore, so I'll just mosey along to rifles and think about "fits the shape of the hand" convenience. Could I build a pot scrubber with a pistol grip? A trigger to shoot soap? And what about a cigarette lighter—could I burn the pot clean? Probably not. But I could make my pot scrubber refillable.

On and on. Once you have some practice at recombinations—which is just what you'll get in spades in the following chapter—you could walk up and down the aisle of a grocery store, jotting down dozens of creative ways to make a better pot scrubber.

Then what? What does Jim Bangel do once he's "searched the world"? How does he turn the raw material of invention—recombination—into a finished idea?

I had to overcome the stereotype of the scientist who sits alone in his laboratory and three years later emerges with his discovery. I force myself to spend two to three hours a day in conversation. I must get up and walk around the building or I'm not doing my job. I provide, at best, ten to fifteen percent of the solution to a problem. Another person provides another ten or fifteen percent and suddenly we have a one hundred percent solution.

Notice that the entire Bangel process is the opposite of sitting alone in the dark, waiting for inspiration. Bangel is no waiter; he is an explorer.

■ HAVING SPOKEN about a quotidian kitchen gadget, I'd like to turn to a grander pursuit: architecture. Doing so, I intend to demonstrate that potscrubber creativity is quite the same as skyscraper creativity.

One of the most provocative buildings of the past decade is the AT&T Building in New York, designed by Johnson and Burgee Architects. *The New York Times* called the building "pleasing, even exciting to look at, as opposed to the dreary towers of a previous generation of skyscrapers." How did it come about? According to Alan Ritchie, the architect who headed the project, the usual background came first—studying the site, determining the number of square feet needed, meeting with the client, and so forth. One certain conclusion taken from this preliminary work was that the building be distinctive. John DeButts, then AT&T's chairman, leaned across his desk and told the architectural team, "I want an identity, something that stands out. I don't want a cigar box."

Holding in mind what the building could *not* be like (a cigar box), the architects asked themselves *what else it might resemble.* Thinking of how tall and narrow the new building would be, one team member said that the building would be like a column. Now, a column needs something on top of it (for instance, the swirls suggesting rams' horns that are found on Ionic columns). So the architects began drawing various ornamental "caps," inspired by the entire history of columns.

Even if one knows nothing about architecture, I think it is readily apparent that as soon as the imagination is allowed to play with the idea of a "column," many delightful recombinations are accessible. The finished AT&T Building does *not* much resemble a column (indeed, it has been nicknamed "the Chippendale skyscraper" because the roofline looks like the top of a china cabinet); the concept of a column was simply a way to charm the imagination. The creative breakthrough came in response to the search for a new metaphor—if it was not to be a "cigar box," what was it to be like? Someone might have said, "It's like a radio tower," and they would have looked at designs that resemble the TransAmerica building in San Francisco. Someone might have said the building was like a tree, in which case an entirely new set of recombinations would have been available to the imagination.

■ IF YOU WANT MORE EVIDENCE of combinations creativity, tune your TV to "Miami Vice" and you'll see the result of a conscious decision by Brandon Tartikoff, president of NBC's entertainment division, to blend a cops-and-robbers show with the visual and aural style of MTV, the music video channel (itself a simple combination). Or drive down the street and see all the new mini-vans, those offspring of the marriage of a car and a van. Or drink a light beer. Whichever you choose, I believe it will lead you to join me in two conclusions:

- Creativity begins with a notion of what you want to accomplish. Such a goal gives order and purpose to the process. (Perhaps a few former hippies are suddenly skeptical, arguing that order and purpose are contrary to the creative act. I must shout, NO! Does an author who knows the subject of his book stifle his creativity? No, it is the author unclear of purpose who must fail.)
- Those who are creative have acquired a system (often a set of unconscious habits) that produces ideas. This system must, by definition, consist of a procedure to (a) acquire recombinant bits; and (b) juxtapose these to the task at hand. Jim Bangel searching the world for ideas, Allan Ritchie looking for visual metaphors: what they have in common is their willingness to assist the imagination, to go in exploration among new sets of information that can be used to produce new combinations.

(To extend the author analogy I used in the previous point, it's apparent that the writer who knows the rules of grammar is freer than one who does not, one who muddles along reinventing written sense. The same goes for the inventor who has a system for creativity; he is freer than one who must await some fickle "inspiration." A system for creativity frees the imagination.)

CHAPTER 4

THE IDEA RANCH

—————————■—————————

I have never hesitated to take from other painters anything I want. But I have a horror of copying myself.

Picasso

What should I keep if averages were all?

John Ciardi

I once heard it said that "evolution is God's greatest invention" (a tidy Astaire around the evolution-versus-creationism debate). Certainly there is nothing so inspired, so awesome, so, as James Joyce put it, "scrotum-tightening," as the ingenuity of Nature. Yet think again of how simple a system it is—rather than one creature just dividing to reproduce identical creatures, two creatures unite and produce a third creature that is a *recombination* of the parents' characteristics. Throw in an occasional mutation and soon you have a gene pool capable of infinite variety. Think anew of the creative power of this simple system, of the varieties of fish or birds that it created, think even of the infinite ingenuity with which it re-creates the human nose.

We are going to borrow God's greatest invention

to create ideas. Welcome to Idea Ranch, where we take ordinary thoughts and cross them with greatness.

Breeding Ideas

In this chapter, I want to teach you to cross one career with another of greater or at least complementary accomplishment. It happens in the workplace all the time—the talents of one individual "rub off" on others. But the natural "rubbing off" is too slow, too limited and limiting, too random. . . . How many workers are rubbing against *greatness*? And of those lucky few, how many have a diversity of greatness from which to choose, optimizing the evolution of their talents? No one I know. But such diverse genius does exist in two places: bookstores and libraries.

A good book is more than paper and ink; it is a great mind for you to open and search. What a profound power it is to walk up to a shelf of books and to pick and choose among minds, to approach them at one's own pace and to embrace them or cast them aside at will. A bookstore or library is a genetic pool—innovations, solutions, styles, and personality traits—available for recombination with you and your career. You can evolve yourself! No need to wait upon finding a "mentor," no need to let fate decide who will "rub off" on you. You not only choose who influences you, but *when* and *how* you are influenced.

Remember the new pot scrubbers I described in the previous chapter? How I took diverse products and tried to borrow their attributes? Doing so, I sought to marry two familiar products and produce new, better ones as offspring. In this chapter we will do likewise with careers.

Perhaps it isn't overly corny to describe the process this way: If you want to learn history, put yourself in the shoes of great men; if you want to make history, put great men in your shoes. This is a simplification, of course—we have seen the dangers of imitation, no matter how admirable the template. I once read that "to steal from one source is plagiarism, to steal from many is research." We aren't going to steal anything— how can you steal genius?—but we are going to research our geniuses well.

We're going to take the grim business of problem-solving and make it the entertainment of a lifetime. Think of how hilarious, and how profoundly educational, it would be if Tom Jefferson showed up in your office and took over your assignment for a while. How would he get things done? How quickly could he overcome the problems? How about Napoleon? Martin Luther King, Jr.? Golda Meir?

Does the notion strike you as ridiculous? Think how you felt when you first heard about evolution. There is something about recombination that is awkward and funny; but there is nothing more natural, no force more powerful. With idea evolution you can, in a matter of hours, breed hundreds of solutions to any given problem, and, in a matter of days, produce a catalog of creativity, an entire career-acceleration guidebook. And the guidebook you produce will be yours alone, matched by you to your goals.

In the first pages of this book I promised you that I would not tell you how to live your life, not offer you a mold into which you would pour your career, but that I would teach you to be a maker of molds. Idea evolution is how I will keep that promise.

The Idea Ranch

Here are my preliminary recommendations for idea evolution. (This is a brief overview of the procedure; we will work through a number of examples in this chapter, and only then do I expect that the mechanics of the system will be clear to you.)

1. If you aspire to being different, unique, and innovative, you must look to people with such traits. While you may have one or two individuals from your own life who seem to you to have the qualities necessary to produce creative solutions, I urge you to also turn to books.

2. As for which books, try going into your local library or bookstore and peruse the biographies section. Remember you are looking for an honest account of the attitudes and actions of someone who, if put in your place, would surely *shake things up, cause some excitement.*

3. Having found some likely-looking books, read them with a pen in your hand. Copy down whatever passages strike you as interesting. On your first reading do not attempt to apply these interesting passages to your own life, simply generate a list. Some people note several passages per page, some a few per chapter, and some only a handful in an entire volume. I would suggest that you be generous

with your ink and note every *action or attitude* that seems to you to be *surprising*—note anything that strikes you as something you would not have said or done. (Remember that our goal is recombination—if your reaction to a deed is, "That's what I would have done," then it doesn't represent an opportunity for creativity. Apples plus apples equals a lousy fruit stand.)

4. When you have finished the first reading of the book, you will have assembled a number of out-of-the-ordinary actions and attitudes. It is then time to try to apply each one to your particular circumstance. Many of the ideas or actions you've noted will be worthy of emulation. That's fine. But keep in your mind a picture of those silly imitators who tried to fly by imitating birds, by wearing wings and jumping off the barn roof . . . we want more than imitation. We will achieve it by redefining, by repeatedly returning to the seed idea and asking, childlike, why? Why did it work? (Again, think back to my example in the previous chapter of the pot scrubber, in which I bred the idea of a pot scrubber with the idea of convenience. Recall, for instance, that we didn't literally imitate the pop-top, but we asked ourselves *why* the pop-top was successful.)

5. Once you have developed a facility for generating ideas, don't rest—keep breeding, looking for further, more refined, generations of ideas. Try to pair your best ideas with all the others.

I am sure that these recommendations now seem somewhat remote and academic, perhaps even confusing. For this reason I am going to take three lives and show you how each would begin a set of career-acceleration ideas. I've chosen three diverse career situations—a sales manager, a "junior executive," and an entrepreneur.

The Evolution of a Sales Manager

Make sure you're comfortable. Put your feet up. Get yourself something to drink. All right.

We are going to begin by evolving the career of a conscientious and ambitious young sales manager, a man who mistakenly believes he has hit an impasse in his career. (I have chosen a sales manager for my demonstration so that we can consider two vital fields at once, sales and management.)

For simplicity's sake, let me call this fictitious character Peter, and say that Peter's life goal is to be a star in his present, rather narrow career, the film-rental business. Before we begin with the evolution, let me give you enough background on Peter for you to understand what success means to him and what his present job consists of.

Peter's present employer has rights to distribute films for several of the nation's leading movie makers, renting them to organizations that are not in the business of showing movies, such as schools and churches. The company for which Peter works has three regional offices, including the one in Dallas that Peter heads, and it enjoys a steady demand for its films.

Our young manager loves film and, for the most part, his job. But he feels stymied—he has no chance of promotion without leaving his beloved Dallas; he markets the company's services to a fairly small, stable client base that seems to hold small promise of sales growth and, hence, little chance of expansion of his regional office or his salary; and he senses his work settling into monotony.

Peter has a staff of three sales representatives, a secretary, and a film librarian (responsible for mailing the selected film to the renter). At present, the sales effort consists of distributing a film catalog and taking orders over a toll-free telephone number. When time permits, the order-takers become salespeople and call existing accounts with film ideas, or place calls to potential accounts. These order-takers/salespeople tend to be recent college graduates who are willing to take a low-pressure job with regular hours in exchange for a modest salary.

Peter's principal success strategy has been to closely observe the owner of the company and try to emulate his cool, detached, and somewhat casual professional style. (Naturally, the other regional managers and most of the headquarters personnel are also imitating the owner's style and thus Peter is one of many impersonators.)

What we have, in sum, is a fairly ordinary young man in a fairly ordinary sales-management dilemma. Let's cross him with greatness and see if we can't evolve for him an armful of new ideas that would increase the performance of his office, provide him with some individuality, and make him one of the most influential young men in the company.

We begin by going into a local bookstore and studying the biography titles in search of someone who, put in Peter's shoes, would make those shoes fly. The first book we open is one about Vince Lombardi (George F. Flynn's *The Vince Lombardi Scrapbook*, an oversized paperback that happens to be on the sale table).

Why Vince Lombardi?, you might ask. Our chief prerequisite is that the biography be of a man who would *shake things up*. Lombardi took the worst team in pro football and made it the greatest team ever. That's the sort of shake-up we want for Peter. Further, we know that our sales manager's present style of management is casual. Although our goal is not to simple-mindedly invert whatever is current, it seems likely that a much different style, a tough-guy style, might make a good cross for our breeding of ideas. Actually, the subtleties of selection are not critical. For the moment, as good a reason as any for picking Lombardi would be that his biography happened to be on the sale table. Do not forget that our intention here is *not* to find a hero, an idol to worship or emulate, but just to shop for some *attributes* of greatness that Peter might don as he evolves his successful self.

Nor should we embark upon this task thinking that by reading a single biography, we'll be able to accurately predict what a Lombardi would have done in Peter's position. In a way, what Lombardi *actually* would have done in that position is not important. You and I know that he lived and died without ever having been a sales manager for a film-rental company. So don't be disturbed if you cannot say with certainty what Lombardi would have done; that does not matter. We are not going to *be* Lombardi, we are going to borrow a bit of his greatness.

Vince Lombardi, Regional Sales Manager

PARENT IDEA

The first item to catch my eye was that Lombardi frequently got the team on their knees and led them in prayer.

OFFSPRING

If Peter believes in prayer, and knows how employees share that predilection, he could begin a similar practice. But if this literal translation of Lombardi's prayerfulness does not suit Peter, let's not be too quick to abandon it. We start by asking, why? Why might a team prayer have helped? Oh, perhaps it united the players and at the same time provided a sense of destiny and purpose.

Okay. How could Peter imitate the success without actually imitating the action? What other forms of mutual endeavor might be akin to a prayer? Peter's version of a "team prayer" might be a morning meditation, a daily pep talk, or a daily exercise program. Or perhaps a better secular translation of the "team prayer" concept is the establishment of some office ideal, a philosophy. Or some old-fashioned cheerleading might be useful—Peter could work up a motto or slogan that could serve as a rallying cry.

I'm not doing too well—these ideas aren't getting

me excited. I'd better turn childlike and get my creative half cranked up. Let's start over. "Why a team prayer?" I ask as innocently as a five-year-old. "To ask for God's help," I reply.

"Why are we asking for help?" This forces me to a new answer: "Because it's really important they do their best."

"Why?"

I am forced to confront reasons why a film rental company can be sufficiently significant to catch the divine eye. This leads me to think of employees earning a living in order to support families. Aha! Families!

I start thinking about families. I think of children's birthday parties as a potential new source of rental business. I think of "family film festivals" as a good way to help Peter's school or church customers promote their fundraising use of films. Perhaps, I decide, Peter should send with the films some little "scorecards" and ask children and parents to rate films shown during the "family film festival." He could tally the results and create some "Family Academy Awards" for which he could get free publicity or promote himself in order to rent more films to other customers.

Now I'm excited.

I hear some of you asking, "But why did you go from prayer to the idea of families? Couldn't you have gone in a hundred directions?" Exactly the point of this book!

FURTHER APPLICATIONS

For the sake of your own career, take a minute to consider why anyone would take an interest in you or the operation you manage. If you're stumped for an answer, then you know you've been running a management-by-limitation shop. Time to experiment. You might start by setting for yourself the goal of heading the department that is one of the most sought-after places of employment in your company or in your city. How to do that? Ask yourself, what is it that your employees love? You might ask *them* what they would rather do than work. Then you set out to incorporate some elements of passion into their jobs.

If the above process seems implausible, that's evidence that you have been in line too long. Let me show you. . . .

Say you are a young woman who manages assembly-line workers. There's a high turnover of employees, a fact that puzzles you. Your firm offers a competitive wage and benefits package. And since you read *The One Minute Manager*, "feedback" is your middle name. But that hasn't helped. You ask some of your employees to go out for a drink after work and you ask them why. "The job stinks," they tell you. "Boring. Mindless." "But," you reply, shaken, "don't I give you lots of one-minute appraisals?" "Yep," they say, "you tell us all the time just how well we do our boring, mindless work." Mentally backpedaling, you ask the workers about money: "Don't we have a competitive wage and benefits package?" They tell you, "Sure. 'Competitive' means you pay just what everybody else pays." And so you are stumped. You finally get so angry that you blurt out, "Well, what big-deal things would you do if you weren't working, smarty-pants?"

They think you're serious. One says he wants to

keep up with current events. A couple say they want to spend more time with their families. A couple more say they hate missing daytime television.

What can you do? Put a big-screen television in the lunch room? Too expensive? You don't want a television around? Perhaps you do your own "program" each morning by letting the workers take turns doing readings from novels or from the newspaper. (Since I first wrote this section I have learned that the old Cuban cigar factories in Florida had "readers" who spent their days walking among the workers with newspaper or book in hand.)

Does my example now seem too easy? What about those who said "spend more time with their families"? Perhaps part of the work can be done at home. Perhaps special "school hours" shifts could be set up. Maybe you could have the school bus stop at the plant and the kids ride home with their parents. And so forth. The secret here is to look at elements of work life and family life and see where the two could be made to intersect.

PARENT IDEA

One of the characteristics Lombardi's players frequently recalled was his perfectionism. There was a feeling that no mistake escaped him. The effect of this was to demand the players' all on every play in every game, and even in every practice. This was part of Lombardi's conception of "thinking like a champion."

OFFSPRING

Our sales manager might want to consider demanding perfection. He could go over every form, every letter and find the smallest mistakes, every typo and grammatical error. So much for imitation. Can we do better?

We start with our "why" questions and, doing so, we just might deduce that Lombardi's perfectionism worked because he was able to diagram for each player exactly *what* to do and demonstrate *how* to do it; then, using game films, he could *compare* each performance to the ideal.

Peter's salespeople are in their offices on the phone and Peter is never certain what they are doing. If Peter asked the sales force to record some of their calls, he would then be able to play back the calls and make suggestions. If he were to follow Lombardi in this, he would call his department together and play the tapes of each salesperson in front of the others. He would then dissect each call, making suggestions. All the salespeople would benefit from hearing their colleagues in action and from the "coaching."

But what if Peter wanted to "coach" personal sales calls outside the office? He might rent some video-tape equipment and do mock sales calls, enabling his salespeople to see themselves in action. He might even ask prospective customers to come in and participate in the rehearsal sales.

FURTHER APPLICATIONS

No one in our sports-oriented society needs to be told what skillful coaching can mean to a team. But we nonetheless fail to learn from coaches. All we know about coaches are the "personality profiles" we get on television, so we think that charisma is the secret of coaching. But the most successful coaches are the innovators, the ones who come up with new exercise regimens, new defenses, better ways to monitor performance. If you want to learn from coaches, pay attention to the behind-the-scenes details, not to personality. You might learn, for instance, that the coach of the University of Houston's basketball team hired an N.B.A. star to come and work with his players on free-throw shooting. Now that's something tangible with which to breed ideas. Who is the equivalent of an N.B.A. star in your industry? Maybe you could get the best car salesman in the state to spend an evening with your salespeople. Or maybe you break the sales job into separate skills (just as a coach might do), and you hire a voice coach, an acting coach, a writing coach. (This needn't be expensive—the "coaches" could be professors from a nearby college who each work with you one afternoon a month.)

PARENT IDEA

Vince Lombardi *hated* to lose. He took every point scored against his team as a personal affront.

OFFSPRING

How can our sales manager figure out when he's losing? Peter may realize that he doesn't "know the score"; is he losing to his competition? He might need to hire a research company to survey his clients. I know of a truck-rental company that hires individuals to go and stand beside given highways on given days and count the number of rental trucks that go by. (That same company had a president so obsessed with beating the competition that he had decals of competitors' logos made up and sent them to his sales offices with instructions to mount them in the office urinals . . . so that the salesmen could literally "piss on the competition.")

Surely Vince Lombardi made it his business to know what had gone wrong on every point scored against him. Could our sales manager do the same? He could call a lost account, explain that he wanted his company to do better in the future, then conduct a brief interview. In this way he could not only find any mistakes his own salespeople made, but might spot ways his competitor's effort was superior. He might also learn of any weaknesses in his product line or in his promotions or pricing. If he has complete records on every lost sale, he might persuade headquarters to make changes. Think of the difference between (a) whining to headquarters that the product is inferior; and (b) showing headquarters a complete list of accounts that could have been, including a dollar total of lost sales.

But these hate-to-lose ideas are just two of the many paths Peter could have followed. Perhaps he might have thought of *scoreboards*, and begun a different path of evolution.

FURTHER APPLICATIONS

The sales function is one in which the competition is apparent and measurable. But do not believe that other departments cannot benefit from a scoreboard. If you manage an accounting department, you might decide you want to be recognized as the finest accounting department in the city. That means competition. That means regularly and systematically taking the time to find out how you and others are doing. You might begin keeping relevant statistics on your scoreboard—compare to other firms the number of accounting personnel per million dollars of sales. If comparisons to other companies are difficult, you can compete with yourself—you might keep score on how many days elapse from the close of an accounting period until publication of results.

In one of my first jobs, with a consumer products company, we periodically tested the appeal of new product ideas. We accomplished this testing by stopping shoppers in a mall, asking them to read a "concept board" (which resembles a preliminary magazine ad), and then asking them how likely they would be to buy the new offering. The company believed that a certain percentage of consumers had to say they would try the new product in order for it to continue investing in the product's development. Out of curiosity, I searched the company records and compiled a history of these "purchase intent" scores. I spotted there our corporate blunders, saw the high scores given to product ideas that went on to be expensive test-market *failures*. Clearly we had a faulty scoreboard. I found inconsistencies in our test procedures that were causing the problem, and made adjustments that standardized the old scores. Then, whenever new scores came in, I inserted them into the historical list. I was no longer content just knowing that a score was good or bad; I had to know what ideas it beat and didn't beat. Not only were the scores more accurate, but they were put in the proper context . . . same old data, new scoreboard.

I'd like to pause to comment on the process we are involved in. The human mind is quite skilled at finding similarities, at defining "what something is like." It has been said that the greatest accomplishment of any individual is to learn language. And it has also been said that language is nothing but metaphor—that we can only describe something by saying what it is like. Thus, to live is to practice metaphor creativity, and metaphor creativity is what you get when you ask, what is it like?

To this point I have taken three sentences from the Lombardi biography and turned them into dozens of ideas for Peter to add to his career-acceleration notebook. He might think that, by and large, the ideas were unexceptional. That's okay—we're just getting loosened up. Peter could produce a hundred ideas from the Lombardi exercise. And if he pursues just five, he's still five ahead of every peer. And, as we shall see, this is only the first generation of ideas; the initial ideas will beget yet more ideas.

Although there are many other Lombardi facts, ideas, and personality traits that could be explored for Peter's benefit, I'm an impatient man and I'm eager to play with a new set of recombinations.

Sigmund Freud, Regional Sales Manager

One leading candidate for Most Influential Thinker in the past century is Sigmund Freud. As a pleasing contrast to the tough and physical Vince Lombardi, let us see if we can take a piece or two of film-rental advice from Freud.

PARENT IDEA

One of Freud's earliest breakthroughs was in his work with paralysis, hallucinations, and other symptoms of hysteria. Hysteria was once generally regarded as a short circuit in the brain, or as an "imaginary" illness, or even as witchcraft. Many researchers failed to identify any physical reason for the symptoms, and it was regarded as incurable. Yet Freud identified psychological causes—repressed memories—and began work on cures.

OFFSPRING

Like any good explorer, Freud was attracted to that which was thought to be impossible. Fertile ground for new ideas is the *idea junkyard*. Many ideas that previously failed did so due to poor execution, not to the inherent wrongheadedness of the idea. Knowing this, Peter might begin to explore his company's old files to find out what has been attempted and to figure out why it failed or succeeded. His goal might soon be to present a theory for what works and what doesn't.

But how else might Peter evolve Freud's hysteria findings? He might decide to investigate *causes*. For Peter this means understanding (a) why customers rent or don't rent films; and/or (b) why they rent them or don't rent them from Peter. He would begin to read the existing literature on the psychology of film and try to understand the underlying factors that make films successes or failures. This very undertaking would give him something to discuss with clients, former clients, and nonclients, and might even result in some usable analysis that would change the way he and his salespeople thought about the rent-or-not-to-rent decision. He might share such findings with the home office and even establish himself as the company's authority on the likely success of different films. Such a reputation might involve him in greater contact with the company's top management and, eventually, with filmmakers. Peter might even aspire to being the nation's leading authority on why films succeed.

FURTHER APPLICATIONS

Spend a little time in the corporate graveyard—you know, all those big metal filing cabinets out in the hall. Often the information in those files cost millions of dollars to collect, but, having served its immediate purpose, it now sits forgotten. A rookie employee who spends a little time with the files can know more about the company than those with a decade of seniority. And if you have a detective's bent, you can do much more than collect anecdotes; you can be the first to find patterns in the mistakes and successes.

I already related the story of how my own time in the files allowed me to improve a company's new-product-evaluation procedures; but I had other file-room triumphs, including a new pricing system that put an extra million in the company's profit pocket. The company I then worked for had a complicated pricing system whereby the same product sold for different prices in different cities. (The price was driven by local supply conditions.) I used the price and sales data to draw a demand curve, just like in

Econ 202, but with real data. It illustrated the fact that demand was inelastic—that is, it was not sensitive to changes in price—and the company confidently put through a 20 percent across-the-board price increase.

PARENT IDEA

Dr. Freud has written that anti-Semitism was ultimately *useful* to him, steeling him for adversarial situations and accustoming him to being in a minority.

OFFSPRING

Our sales manager might explore ethnocentricity and decide to, say, put together a package of Mexican films to promote in Hispanic communities. He might from there rediscover market segmentation. Should he notice that sales are particularly strong (or particularly weak) among a given denomination—Baptists, for example—he might want to put together a special brochure in which program directors at some of the area's best known Baptist churches are quoted, with sample programs provided. He might steal a page from the Baptists themselves and declare a Baptist membership campaign in which he contacts every Baptist church in his sales territory with a special promotional package. (I remember reading of a minister who had established a Ten Most Wanted List—the ten influential citizens he thought would be of greatest benefit to his church as members. Peter might do likewise; surely a Ten Most designation would flatter a prospective customer, particularly if his name appeared alongside those of other community leaders.)

As for Freud's suggestion that being a minority thickens one's skin, perhaps Peter might consider the advantages of directly challenging his larger competitors, promising to beat their prices or to cut their delivery time in half.

But if we ask ourselves why anti-Semitism proved useful to Freud, we eventually must return to the idea of difference. Freud was accustomed to being unusual, to standing apart. If our sales manager is a WASP, perhaps he should move into a Jewish neighborhood, or start attending a Black church. Crazy? Probably. But somehow a person who is to be better must grow accustomed to being different. Another way to do this is to spend some time out on a limb, some time undertaking projects that seem to all those around him destined to fail. For this he might employ the "opposites" approach and ask himself which are the hardest films to rent or what is the worst potential market. Having done so, Peter might find a new twist—perhaps he might try to promote the company's worst films, even starting a Bad Films series, in search of America's least favorite movie.

FURTHER APPLICATIONS

Two ideas emerged from Freud's remark about anti-Semitism: market segmentation and skin-thickeners. About the first of these, let me add one observation. Over the years that I have tested new product ideas and new advertisements, I have seen my clients spend fortunes relearning the same lesson: If you design a product for Everyman, you'll sell it to no one.

That's simply saying what everyone knows to be true—you can't please everybody. To try is folly. Try to create music that everyone will like and what do you get? Muzak. And the only way you could possibly please every superior, every peer, every relative, is to attempt nothing. And then what do they think of you? A zero, a wimp, a nerd. You might as well get used to criticism.

Which brings me to the second part of our anti-Semitism discussion. I started to write that one could fill the encyclopedia with stories of those who undertook "crazy" ideas and made them work, but then I realized that the encyclopedia is very nearly just that. The history of progress is the history of defying conventional wisdom. Every time a person feels out of place, he or she is getting in some practice at being different. Where do you feel out of place? Go there and *don't* try to fit in. Revel in being an outsider. Then go back to where you work and take a stand, oppose the majority, and make them love it.

PARENT IDEA

A pattern that emerges as one studies Freud's career is that he was something of an intellectual bandit. The name Freud stands alone above names like Fliess or Koller or Breuer or Charcot or Borne, even though the names just cited were the originators of some of Freud's most important theories. Why is it, then, that we remember Freud more than the others? Because Freud would seize the ideas and give eloquent voice to them. He would publish articles and give speeches about the idea and, while he gave credit to its originator, it somehow always ended up being remembered as "Freud's idea."

This may seem contradictory to the explorer mentality, but it is not. While Freud took the ideas from others, he took them from men who were unlikely to publish them or who were more interested in other areas of exploration. He was thus able to possess the idea alone.

OFFSPRING

The notion of becoming an intellectual bandit may be unappealing. But Freud did not push his colleagues out of the way, did not bully them; he simply took up their batons and carried them farther and faster than they might have. Borrowing this notion, our sales manager could set up a surveillance campaign designed to grab new ideas. Peter could, for instance, take an international approach, contacting film companies in Europe, Asia, or elsewhere, trying to get copies of their catalogs or sales material, and hoping to exchange correspondence with those in positions similar to his own but in different environments. Those colleagues in different environments might have produced different solutions which, while ordinary overseas, might be considered revolutionary in the U.S. Peter could also set up some system to monitor the innovations of his competitors, using the loyal clients as a source.

Finally, if Peter were to become sincere about developing ideas and were to establish a reputation as the sort of motivated employee who could take a good idea and turn it into positive business results, he would become a magnet for new ideas. Top management would be likely to call Peter when they had an idea they wanted tested. The experimenter attracts experiments: *not only does he seek ideas, they seek him*. Realizing this, Peter must ask himself how he could develop a reputation as an "idea man." This would begin a whole new evolution of ideas on making himself the center of experimentation. Having read about Freud, he would start by knowing that he can simply get ideas from less ambitious or energetic peers or from his superiors. He need only call other executives in the company and engage them in a discussion of possible experiments. Those with ideas will thank Peter for doing something with them.

Or Peter might get five or ten of his clients together for a group discussion on how he could better serve them, and use their opinions to generate new programs and to persuade his management to help implement them.

FURTHER APPLICATIONS

Keep in mind what was said earlier: people tend to judge you according to your goals. Make it clear that you are willing to experiment, and experiments will find you.

I know one chap who, as a junior executive, put a Suggestion Box on his door and published the offerings in a monthly memo. Many were suggestions only in the most appallingly literal sense—you can imagine the vile jokes he received—but this served only to heighten interest in his monthly memo. All of a sudden, his office door was on the corporate map.

Ask those who use your work how it could be of more use to them. Even if they don't have any ideas, they will be grateful for the question. It might just start them thinking. And don't expect that they will just dump more tasks upon you. My experience suggests quite the opposite; most people aren't very good at envisioning something that they don't have at that point, but they are quite certain of what they have that they don't need. I have had clients tell me that I was doing three times as much work as I needed to; that, indeed, all the superfluous work was just clogging up the system. Why didn't they tell me sooner? Anyone who has worked in a large organization knows the answer: no one ever asked.

We are only beginning to explore Peter's possibilities, but I must stop here; I could fill this volume you're holding with suggestions for him. Indeed, I would suggest to Peter that he fill his own volume, doing a complete idea evolution program with many more "Parent Ideas" from each biography he selects. I'd urge him not to stop generating ideas until he had a catalog of genius from which to select a new success approach—until he was certain he had *many more ideas than he could use.*

But for fear of growing repetitious or having you suspect that my system for breeding ideas is limited to a sales manager or to film rentals, let us move on to a new situation.

The Corporate Elevator

Let us now turn our attention to a young woman I will call Lisa, who, for the sake of simplicity, will have only one goal in life: to head the large advertising agency for which she works. For easy reference, let's pick a name (or, more in keeping with the pattern for agency names, a set of initials) for her firm: G/B/U. Lisa is one year out of college and is presently an assistant account executive, meaning she is one of several people responsible for working with one of G/B/U's important clients. Her superior, the account executive, is a team leader, rather like a quarterback, and is responsible for charming the agency's clients—as well as coordinating the efforts of the various departments responsible for producing the ads and seeing that they reach the public. There are hundreds of details that the account executive must attend to—from listening to the new contract demands of the product's Hollywood spokesperson, to making sure the client's mother has special passes to get into "The Tonight Show."

Lisa is in the dawn of her career; she has no subordinates or influence. Her career is in an awkward growth stage—she has learned the rudiments of her job but receives only beginner's assignments. She is ready to advance before the company is ready to advance her. It is a difficult period in anyone's career, when the early fascination of a job and the pleasure of the first real salary have worn thin and the corporate pyramid looms beyond the seeing. Lisa is in need of some adventure, some passion, some exploration.

I have selected two idea partners for Lisa, exciting personalities whom I chose because I thought she might have chosen them for herself.

Barbara Jordan,
Assistant Account Executive

The former Congresswoman from Texas, Barbara Jordan, is a fascinating contemporary success story. Let's see what we can learn from her book, *Barbara Jordan: A Self-Portrait.*

One of the first interesting statements I encountered was Ms. Jordan's adolescent vow, "I'm not going to be like the rest." Ah, how many of us say that! Before we get into our evolving procedure, let's think again about the quality of being unlike the rest.

"I'm not like the rest," Lisa might now whisper to herself as she walks into her boss's office and asks her where she buys her suits. And as she watches the suave Chairman of the Board speak at the annual Employees' Dinner, she tumbles to the insight that she is not going to be like the rest—oh, no, she is going to be just like G/B/U's chairman. How quickly the path to success becomes crowded! So let us hope for Lisa that when she says, "I'm not going to be like the rest," she actually goes about it by being different.

Lisa might begin by taking an inventory of what she is accepting without question. She should try to write down the tenets of the "Gospel According to G/B/U." What do all the rest believe? What idols do they bow before? If she is going to be different, she should start by realizing what it means to be the same.

Roger Myers, the sharp-witted vice president and creative director of Burch Myers Cuttie Advertising in Chicago, actually did write something similar. His article, "What Do Those Pitches in New Business Presentations Really Mean?", listed clichés that advertising agencies use in their meetings with prospective client firms. An example:

> Pitch: Rather than take up your time with our speculations and guesses about your particular advertising needs, we've decided to use this time to provide you with a general overview that will help you appreciate our experience, resources and capabilities.

> Translation: We're going to show you a canned presentation.

Creative minds are interested in clichés—how can you be sure you're ungrooved unless you know the grooves?

PARENT IDEA

The school activity to which Ms. Jordan devoted herself was the debate team. She also entered every speaking contest she could, knowing that the ability to speak to a group would be useful.

OFFSPRING

Lisa is required to make presentations to clients, and perhaps she secretly dreads every one. If so, she must not just "overcome" her aversion (there's that mountain-climber mentality again), but she must find a means to embrace speaking, to be passionate about it. So, she could find a class or club devoted to improving one's facility for speaking. A good idea. But because Lisa is always looking for an unconventional approach, perhaps she can make this a *great* idea by making it different. Every successful account executive can do a competent speech-class presentation. Lisa must look for instruction *outside* a class. She could learn to feel comfortable giving speeches by becoming a mime or a clown, or by going to acting school, or by auditioning for roles in local plays. Perhaps she should sit in on coaching sessions for the mock trials at a local law school, or audit the homiletics (that is, sermon-giving) class at a nearby seminary. Not only could she learn about communication in any of these ways, but she could, at the same time, broaden herself and acquire some ear-grabbing anecdotes to tell at all those agency-client luncheons.

Thinking of those all-important client get-togethers—luncheons, drinks after a presentation, or dinner out—might lead Lisa to conceive of them as a special public-speaking skill. Looking for an unconventional approach, she might ask herself who would be the perfect business lunch companion. If she named a comedian, she might try to meet some of the city's young comedians. She might do this by suggesting a humorous campaign for one of the agency's clients, and thereby make meeting comedians a part of her job. She might convince the agency to utilize the writing skills of her favorite comedian, and, in exchange, ask the comic to teach her what he or she knows about comedy.

FURTHER APPLICATIONS

Every job task, even those that seem insignificant, should be analyzed. You might start by listing your five *least* favorite tasks and try to find a way to romance each one. Maybe you hate filling out forms. One company I worked for had a fleet of cars for employees' business use and a form to fill out every time you returned one. A nuisance? Not for one of my co-workers who, upon returning the Chevette they always gave him, would complete the "Comments?" section with remarks such as "Tends to lose stability over 120 mph." The challenge is not to let bureaucratic tasks turn your mind into gray flannel. Think of the reputation you'll get: a maverick, someone to be watched.

Two other tasks that can be detestable are (1) travel; and (2) "cold call" selling. When I once found myself working for a consulting firm in financial trouble, I volunteered to become a Willy Loman, on the road, making calls only slightly warmer than 32 degrees. When I got sick of it, I wrote a twelve-minute pitch, borrowed a tape recorder, and started sending out my message on cassette tape, along with a package of materials. Then I'd follow up with the serious prospects.

PARENT IDEA

Once she had passed the bar exam and set up an office, our ambitious neophyte attorney was confronted with the old question: where to get clients? She reasoned that her best prospects were those who (1) were likely to need legal help, but who (2) did not at present have a lawyer. She made regular visits to

Good Hope, a nearby charitable organization where the helpless look for help, and handed out business cards.

OFFSPRING

Because Lisa is part of a large agency, one of a team of account executives assigned to serve a large existing account, she might fail to realize the importance of new accounts and fail to learn the skill of acquiring them. But how to gain such experience without being involved in a conflict-of-interest with her present job?

Barbara Jordan, for all her brilliance and ambition, was not too proud to go to Good Hope; our account executive should not be too proud to volunteer her time to some organization such as the Small Business Administration. By volunteering to help small businessmen set up advertising programs, she might be in a position to direct some small accounts to her agency, or, if G/B/U does not appreciate such small accounts, she could refer that business to small agencies (and thereby earn the gratitude of the people she most respects in those agencies).

As always, explorers are not willing to content themselves with imitation, but insist on making good ideas sire great ones. Lisa might decide to donate her time and ideas to G/B/U's new business department. She might ask herself, how could a large agency learn from the Good Hope technique? That appears to be a tough one, and let's pretend it has us stumped. *Why* did Jordan go to Good Hope? Hmmm. Well, as we noted before, the down-and-out are likely to need legal help and are unlikely to already have a lawyer to turn to; Good Hope is a natural meeting place for those likely to need legal assistance, and also a place in which there is little competition among lawyers. Further, an ambitious young attorney seeks not only cases, but cases with the potential for establishing a reputation. What wealthy man would give an important case to a beginner?

How did the down-and-out get to be that way? They're down-and-out because they fell on hard times. Why did they fall on hard times? Perhaps because they weren't educated or found themselves in a dying industry. (We're well into my examples of breeding ideas, and I hope by now you can see what's coming. Take a few minutes and think about what you can make of this down-and-out syndrome. How might you find the corporate equivalents of Good Hope? My answer follows—I hope yours is even better.)

I thought first about companies near bankruptcy. Could companies that are reorganizing be a good market? If the agency develops expertise in promoting new starts and offers such companies an advertising firm that understands their special needs, it could provide an invaluable service and find clients where there isn't any competition. Our explorer might search the *Wall Street Journal* for stories of companies in trouble, or simply ask a stockbroker to compile a list of those firms that have undergone a sizable drop in stock prices over the past months or years. Surely a large percentage of those companies would be looking for help, for ideas, for new advertising.

Some short-sighted individuals might object to such a plan, arguing that troubled corporations would be the least likely to pay their bills. These difficulties could certainly be surmounted: bills could be settled in advance, or bank guarantees issued, or some other plan that financing experts could determine.

FURTHER APPLICATIONS

Why invest time and energy in troubled businesses? Why might it be a good idea? Less competition. You might ask yourself, What kind of business is there that my competitors would *not consider* pursuing? This forces you to try to understand how your competitors decide what new business they will pursue. Understanding the parameters of their search may inspire you to explore new territory yourself.

If you apply such a philosophy to real estate, for instance, you might decide that dilapidated buildings, or ones with tasteless architecture, were of great interest. Indeed, many a real-estate fortune has been made by buying ugly (and hence undervalued) properties, and, after cosmetic changes, selling them at full value.

Or apply the logic to restaurants. One of the country's most successful restaurant chains, Domino's Pizza, began with a contrarian mentality. Thomas Monaghan found that delivery service was something restaurants hated, something they did only until they built sufficient clientele to be able to get along without it. Mr. Monaghan decided not only to specialize in takeout, but he was quick to make it innovative—for example, he put pizza-warming devices in the delivery vehicles.

PARENT IDEA

Besides visiting places like Good Hope, Barbara Jordan volunteered to help in John Kennedy's presidential campaign. She also continued her adolescent vocation of speaking, willing to "speak anywhere on anything."

We witness here how free time can be put to good use. No sitting by the phone praying for it to ring—Jordan was out meeting people, earning respect, getting her name in the paper, and building a reputation for herself even before she had any clients.

OFFSPRING

Why did Barbara Jordan volunteer for a presidential campaign? Lisa might give a cynical answer: she didn't have anything better to do. This may well be the case, and one worth examining. Lisa, instead of competing to work on a glamorous high-visibility account, might ask to be assigned to a staid, undemanding, even dull account, in order to have more time to devote to her self-development. But we can do better. Back to "why"—why was volunteering for Kennedy's campaign useful to Jordan's career? A campaign might be a good source of contacts. Ms. Jordan was probably sufficiently perspicacious to look for contacts outside the normal environment, outside the clubs in which the primary objective of the majority of members is to exchange business cards. So Lisa might want to choose carefully among those campaigns that hold some attraction for her. It would behoove her to know artists, writers, or musicians, as well as businessmen. She might therefore want to devote time to helping the local symphony or art museum or community theater in order to make both kinds of contacts simultaneously.

But let us persist in asking why. Why else might

Barbara Jordan want to make contacts? To look for new business? New careers? New resources for doing her job better? Lisa might realize that contacts in other advertising agencies are quite important. The fastest path to becoming the chairman might take her outside of the agency that happened to need her services when she graduated from college. She could take the conventional route and join the Ad Club and meet other aspiring young agency personnel. Then again, she could innovate. If she were working on a political campaign (or a symphony campaign, or whatever), and got herself on the committee to do advertising and publicity, she would be in a position to ask for help, giving her a reason to meet executives from other agencies.

FURTHER APPLICATIONS

You can probably discern a pattern in all this creativity: it almost always results in work. Glorious, energy-providing, turn-on work . . . but work nonetheless. The simple fact is that if you devote all your "work time" to getting your job requirements completed, you are doomed to being conventional. You have to be in a position to have time to work or after work to innovate.

For instance, George Rupp, Dean of the Harvard Divinity School, told me he mentally stores matters that require contemplation until he needs to take a drive. "The ideas of which I am fondest always seem to come to me in the car," he said. And Roger Myers, the man who wrote the "What Do Those Pitches Really Mean?" article quoted earlier, told me that his best ideas always came outside the office. "If you're stumped," he added, "take a shower."

But turning waste time into productive time can only go so far. You have to be sufficiently creative to find activities that will allow you to develop *and* that your employer will welcome. Find a specialty about which you and your employer can both be passionate. Notice what I have been suggesting for Lisa, the *double duty* of her efforts—she, for instance, wants to develop her presentation skills, so she convinces the agency to consider using young comedians to write or act in commercials; her creativity is in solving two problems at once, her own and her agency's.

If our young executive takes a number of well-considered proposals to her superiors and they repeatedly discourage her initiatives, saying, "It's a good idea, *but* . . . ," then she must consider the possibility that her company will tolerate no getting out of line, wants no disruptions, no excitement, no surprises. If she has succeeded in befriending executives at other agencies, she might seek their counsel: are her proposals worthwhile? If they say no, she can learn how to correct her idea evolution. If they say yes, she may have a new job.

There is, of course, much more to learn from the story of Barbara Jordan; but I think we are ready to journey outside the more conventional boundaries of American success stories and consider the life of a man named John Waters, one of America's most interesting young filmmakers and the author of an autobiography called *Shock Value* (one reviewer called it "the book nobody expected, wanted, or needs"). John Waters is the self-proclaimed "King of Bad Taste," maker of cult films such as *Polyester* and *Pink Flamingoes*, and as his very candid, detailed autobiography makes plain, possessor of a unique career.

John Waters, Assistant Account Executive

PARENT IDEA

Waters succeeded in part because he did *not* do what an aspiring filmmaker should—he did not move to New York or Hollywood, did not curry the favor of the cinematic establishment, did not apprentice himself. No, Waters chose instead to specialize. He chose for himself a genre in which there was little or no competition; he specialized in "trash," what he calls "tasteful bad taste."

OFFSPRING

If we are to ask ourselves on Lisa's behalf how this might apply to an advertising agency, we would learn the by-now-familiar lesson—Waters sought to be different. Moreover, we learn that he sought to be different by *specializing* in a unique area of his industry. Lisa should realize the value of being an expert. There are already hundreds of individuals in the agency who know more about advertising than she does. Yet there are specific elements of advertising in which she could become the agency's recognized authority. If, for example, Lisa had musical ability, she might specialize in advertising jingles. She could put together a library of jingles, collect the musical scores for them, or even try to put characteristics of jingles into a computer and analyze what made them successful.

FURTHER APPLICATIONS

I have already written on the importance of differentiation in a new product or advertisement (and just given the example of Domino's Pizza choosing its specialty), and I hope it is clear that specialization is one way to differentiate a career. But let me say that specialization is most useful when it is a particular strength among strengths ... nobody wants a bad pizza, no matter how fast.

Furthermore, because achievers are explorers hungry for bits of information for recombination, specialization must not make a career narrow, but instead should be like the point on a wedge, allowing other strengths to be brought to bear. Think, for instance, of your last hiring decision. You likely had a line outside your office door of applicants of approximately equal intelligence, experience, and personableness. You had to find some way to break the tie. So you probably took the one who was currently making the least, feeling you could offer a bit lower salary, *unless* one applicant had a particular talent—unless one had a unique ability with statistics, or was a capable cartoonist, or whatever.

PARENT IDEA

When a young John Waters had begun to produce movies, he had to get them shown. He went out and personally persuaded theater owners to do midnight showings of his movies, reasoning that his unique style would appeal to the particular psyche of midnight crowds. In this way, Waters not only made unusual movies, but took an unusual approach to their distribution, pursuing a very special audience.

OFFSPRING

Now here is another opportunity for Lisa to discover *diversity*. Rather than try to appeal to the same general audience for which most corporations battle—the suburban nuclear family—Lisa could seek new markets. These might be new markets for advertising or new markets for her client's products. She would urge her client to think in terms of specialty advertising for special markets (singles, old people, prisoners, prostitutes). But going beyond the obvious, we might ask ourselves, why midnight movies? Such showings are an effort to lengthen the useful hours of theaters. Lisa's mind would also turn to extended uses for products. For example, if her client's product is Jell-O, she would know that the challenge faced by Jell-O is not getting the product into consumers' homes, but getting consumers actually to go to the trouble of making it. An explorer would never simply continue with the old approaches—convincing consumers that Jell-O is good, or providing new recipes—no, a John Waters would think of uses for, say, empty Jell-O boxes. He would put children's prizes on them or invent games using the boxes. Or John Waters might attempt humor, putting together a booklet for "50 Uses for Old Jell-O Boxes," akin to that bestseller about uses for a dead cat.

FURTHER APPLICATIONS

Redefine. Who is your audience and why? There is no occupation where the worker could not learn great lessons by spending some time as the recipient of the work. You probably have heard it suggested that executives call themselves—that is, telephone their own offices using a disguised voice and ask for themselves. How startling to hear what your callers hear: a secretary, voice heavy with ennui, putting you on hold, twice, then yelling down the hall, "Has anybody seen him?", and saying to you, "I guess he isn't here." Find audience equivalents in your job. Try pulling out old memos you wrote, ones so old you don't remember why you wrote them, and read them with a stranger's eye. Go back to the list of attributes of an ideal peer presented in Chapter 2, and see which of those would apply to the author of that memo.

But why diversity? *New* audiences? Who else could use your work? To what new uses could your work be put? The best answer to all these comes from answering yet another question: what problems can you solve? The surest way to someone's respect is to solve one of his or her problems. The conventional employee hides from problems; the explorer searches for them. Where? Eric Von Hipple of MIT analyzed the sources of inventions in scientific equipment and found that, of 160 inventions, over 70 percent came from product users. And Don Young, the chemist/inventor we met earlier, gave me this example: "When I set about finding a way to fix desert soils, to correct them and allow them to be crop land, I went out and worked in the fields."

PARENT IDEA

A paragraph from *Shock Value* demonstrates how the mind of an explorer functions—the asking of endless questions and the willingness to embrace the unusual, even the bizarre. John Waters quotes a newspaper article, citing it as an example of how he gets ideas:

"WOMAN BEHEADS MOTHER, SLASHES OWN THROAT

Police say a woman wished a state trooper 'Merry Christmas' and tossed what authorities said was her mother's head on the sidewalk in front of the New Jersey statehouse. Then the woman pulled out a razor and slashed her own throat."

All sorts of questions pop into mind: Did the head hit anybody? Did it roll and the cops had to chase it?

This is the sort of highly unusual story to which the "King of Bad Taste" would be attracted. But that is not what is interesting about the paragraph, not what proclaims it the work of an explorer. It is the questions that "pop" that should be written in neon. An explorer doesn't merely read the newspaper, doesn't merely react to the stories with sighs or smiles or curses. An explorer doesn't look for answers, but for questions. Ask enough questions and you have your answer. We are conditioned to answer questions as part of our ordinary schooling. Geniuses are askers of questions. Questions are new worlds, answers inhabitants there. To find life on other planets, you must first conceive of other planets.

OFFSPRING

So far my examples have been chosen to be easy to follow and sensible, thus demonstrating how much can be accomplished by a rather dutiful if somewhat plodding manufacturer of ideas (which is what you'll probably be at first). Now that we have warmed up, let's take a minute and take some of the clothes off our imaginations.

Because John Waters is a filmmaker, his mind is always asking for details to help him envision a scene. Because Lisa is in advertising, her mind should always ask for applications to marketing. Let's try to turn even an article on a beheading into useful ideas.

Place Lisa on the account team working on Jell-O. Nothing could be more incongruous, more ridiculous than Jell-O paired with a woman throwing her mother's head to the sidewalk. Preposterous. And, therefore, the start of creativity.

Let us further assume that Lisa wants to assist the creative team in developing new approaches for marketing Jell-O; she is obsessed with the notion of making Jell-O more interesting, more exciting. So, when she reads of the head she thinks of a head and Jell-O together. Here's how her stream-of-consciousness might flow:

> Picture a head inside a big bowl of Jell-O. Horrible. But the idea of putting something interesting inside the Jell-O might be appealing. Perhaps some toy or decoration could be included in the package to put inside the Jell-O (too big to be swallowed, of course, or else edible).

> Perhaps a swimming pool could be filled with Jell-O and people could jump in and eat their way out. Nah. But the publicity department could get some coverage out of the world's largest bowl of Jell-O. *Guinness Book of World Records* stuff.

> Back to the head. Is there some way to make a bust out of Jell-O? Could a series of presiden-

THE IDEA RANCH

tial head molds be created? Is there some sort of flexible mold from which people could make a Jell-O version of their own faces? If some sort of flexible mold is possible—some kind of clay-like substance to wrap around an object—could not then people make Jell-O versions of golf balls or flashlights or what-have-you?

Again, to the head. Could Jell-O cause some excitement by using a murderer as a spokes-woman? Too extreme. But what about using prisoners? Do prisons serve Jell-O? Would they allow the prisoners to comment on camera? If not prisoners, how about seeking out odd users of Jell-O? Odd uses?

FURTHER APPLICATIONS

Whew! I hope you accept the discussion above as proof that once one has become skillful at combining ideas, most any idea will do. In fact, the more extreme the better, in that it may encourage playfulness, an important attribute of the creative mind. John Waters went so far as to say, "I hate reality." This coming from a man who follows weirdos in the street and hangs out in low-rent bars in order to see the "real world." Such ambivalence about reality is not uncommon in artists. They study convention in order to surpass it. While the average man may do something so silly as to want to "get in touch with reality," the genius is searching for the fantastic, looking beyond reality. Reality is everywhere. Reality is ordinary. So Waters seeks the most bizarre forms of reality in order to propel his imagination beyond it.

The person imprisoned by reality would scoff at the serious reflection of how Sigmund Freud would have gone about being a sales manager. "It's unrealistic!" he would cry, and wave away the notion. "Let's get serious," he would demand, and open a Norman Vincent Peale book. He would never suspect that Peale's genius was in envisioning how Jesus Christ would have acted as a sales manager, a fantastic notion in its day.

With that, let us embark upon your last exercise in creativity, generating ideas for a new business.

Creativity and the Entrepreneur

Occasionally a single sentence changes the way one thinks about a subject. This was the case with me and a lone phrase about entrepreneurs. I can still remember vividly both the classroom and the professor as they were on the day I heard this: "The army of small businessmen standing in line to lose their money."

You and I know that if an entrepreneur is to succeed, he must get out of line, particularly the line in which he loses his money. Having considered a salesman/manager and a "junior executive," it will not surprise you that an entrepreneur will use the identical technique to produce ideas. I have chosen a man starting a business that sells the most intangible of products—consulting. In order to lend specificity to our example, I have defined him as opening a consulting firm specializing in banking. I'll call our neophyte consultant Eric, and give him a reasonable background for a consultant—he has worked in two other consulting firms and has a few potential clients. Eric is now in his mid-thirties and has wanted to own his own firm for a dozen years. He has a dream which, for our purposes, can be reduced to building a small but stable and profitable consulting firm.

I suspect you've got the hang of this idea evolution by now, so I will but briefly undertake two pairs of parent ideas, then invite you to take over the final pair.

Daniel Moynihan, Consultant

Rising from a childhood in New York's Hell's Kitchen to become a Harvard professor, an adviser to presidents, Ambassador to the United Nations, and U.S. Senator, Daniel Patrick Moynihan is quite an explorer. Moynihan co-authored a book about his experiences in the United Nations called *A Dangerous Place*. This is the sort of book an idea rancher looks for, for it covers critical years in Moynihan's career and it deals with those years by describing important decisions, including descriptions of why those decisions were made.

PARENT IDEA

Moynihan took it upon himself to keep the President informed of all he did, sending regular reports to the White House. (It was in one of these memoranda that Moynihan used the provocative expression "benign neglect"; a jealous White House staffer leaked the memo to the press.)

135

OFFSPRING

Surely Moynihan would recognize that the President would *not* be interested in having routine reports of the everyday humdrum doings of the U.N., but strictly in notification of debacles about to reach the large ears of some journalist. So was Moynihan merely making work for himself? My guess is that Moynihan was not prompted to help the President remain current on the U.N. as much as he was interested in keeping the President apprised of the name, activities, and achievements of one Daniel Patrick Moynihan. The first step in being influential is being remembered.

Likewise, Eric must be remembered if he is to be hired. He might call all his potential clients every few weeks and ask them, "Any business yet?" (which is exactly how many consultants work). Or he might try to be less direct. Some sort of regular report to his clients and potential clients could be effective. This could take the form of a newsletter or other update on some aspect of banking. If Eric had not the time nor talent to author an impressive newsletter, he might consider making his news a collection of articles he found in other publications, a kind of *Reader's Digest* of banking. Or he might ask clients to contribute articles or consent to interviews.

Before I go into the further applications of these "offspring ideas," allow me to present a related "parent idea."

PARENT IDEA

Moynihan's writing is highlighted by wonderful epigrams. Here is one of my favorites: "Want an audience, start a fight."

136

OFFSPRING

Our ambitious consultant would dearly love an audience, so he might contemplate fights he could start. Here Eric must simply find some issue in banking about which he feels strongly and then begin throwing punches. Or, being creative, Eric might realize that he could start a fight without actually being in it. He could find two individuals who strongly disagree and tape-record a debate between them, which he could then distribute to clients or potential clients. If he felt sufficient interest existed, he might even attempt to organize a seminar or other program that would incorporate the debate.

In asking himself just why the "Want an audience, start a fight" statement was useful, he might concentrate not only on the "fight" but on the "audience." What else attracts an audience? Plays, movies, shopping malls, sports events. Eric might come first upon the weary old idea of buying a block of tickets at some event and offering them to clients. Or he might try to get more participation, organizing a bank-versus-bank softball game or the like. Thinking of the crowds that flock to shopping malls, he might try to put together a "banker's mall"—an assembly in which various services for banks and bankers would be displayed. Thinking of the audiences attracted to movies, Eric might consider making his own film (or at least an audio cassette) about his consulting services. He could ask those clients he had served well to be interviewed and mix this with whatever new consulting approaches he developed.

FURTHER APPLICATIONS

The key that unlocked these ideas is the success of various enterprises in attracting an audience. How does . . . a newspaper? a theater? . . . get and hold its audience? Answer that question and you'll have a dozen ideas for making your career worth noting. What draws a crowd besides a fight? Answer that and you have a new set of ideas to make your work worth looking at.

Indeed, as I thought about Moynihan's ability to attract an audience by use of clever phrase-making, I went back to several of the most clever. A surprise: rarely are they original! But I cannot accuse the Senator of being an intellectual pickpocket—he is too quick-handed to be caught, for he admits, ever so softly, that the statements were borrowed. For example, the "fight" epigram already cited was "taken from the Gaelic." Or, when he wants to perk up a speech, he does it with a vaguely attributed quote, like this dandy: "It is said that if the Communist regime were to take over in the Sahara there would in time be a shortage of sand." Or, when he delivers the marvelous line, "When elephants fight, the grass gets trampled," he precedes it with, "As the Indians say." Senator Moynihan does not steal lines, but neither does he allow us to attribute the epigrams to anyone else.

I would like to propose that every man and woman who reads this book make an effort to apply ideas of audience attraction to business documents, especially interoffice memos; such documents are, to borrow from Oscar Wilde, a "desert of common sense," at best cold and straightforward, at worst bombastic and convoluted. These memos are so dull that a mere five minutes of glancing inside a five-dollar volume of quotations can cause a stir. Imagine starting each memo with a quotation. Say you are inviting managers to a meeting to discuss a bit of bad news about sales. You do it something like this:

> "I don't believe in an afterlife, but I'm taking a change of underwear, just in case."
> —Woody Allen

Please bring a change of underwear to . . .

The 9th floor conference room
Wednesday, September 4
3:00 P.M.

Topic: Christians versus lions. (First quarter sales report.)

Such a memo might take an extra two minutes to prepare. (I found the Woody Allen line by flipping open my desk calendar, which happens to have a "quote of the week.") And think what you could do with an extra hour on a major report—perhaps a bar chart or two, maybe colored ink. I don't mean to be flip; my point is that so little effort is needed in order to make your communications stand apart to increase your audience, your reputation, your effectiveness. Just because a corporation is something born of lawyers doesn't mean that its language must be legalistic. And even though most professions have become besotted with jargon in a pathetic effort to sound "scientific," clarity has never gone out of fashion. If you want an audience, think about what your peers or clients read or watch when no one from work is around. I'll bet it's neither legalistic nor scientific, but rather clear, clever, quick.

Maxwell Perkins, Consultant

Maxwell Perkins is the most famous of all editors, assisting Hemingway and Fitzgerald, among others. He was a friend and confidant of genius, and a genius in his own right, satisfying the very different needs of the leviathan egos of the writers he helped and influenced. From A. Scott Berg's biography, *Max Perkins, Editor of Genius*, we can deduce his secrets of success and evolve ideas for our consultant.

PARENT IDEA

I was surprised to learn that Max Perkins was not a man naturally suited to the job of editor—he was said to be a terrible speller and a slow reader. What overcame this lack of ability for the mechanics of the job was his romance with quality literature, and because of it, his ability to attract and hold writers.

OFFSPRING

Our bank consultant might countenance the possibility that he does not have natural talent for the mechanics of his business. Just as Perkins knew that his real job was not to snip off dangling participles, but to find and encourage brilliance, so might Eric think of his real job as selling not his own capacity for insight, but that of others. Eric could put together a group of professors or talented bank executives and call upon their talents to solve the problems of others. He might choose to promote himself as a clearinghouse for the industry's best minds, or he might prefer to keep his sources anonymous. You don't have to be a genius to sell genius.

FURTHER APPLICATIONS

Weaknesses. What to do with them? The Center for Creative Leadership undertook a study of forty-one top executives and found, according to Randall White, a researcher for the Center, that "all CEOs have flat sides. The most successful ones play to their strengths— and build a staff to cover their weaknesses." Covering weaknesses implies that the CEOs recognized them. It's not easy to hold a mirror to your character. Earlier, I reported the superiority complex of America's youth. Lest you think this afflicts only students, a survey of college faculty revealed that 94 percent rate themselves as above average.

One way to finesse the battle with inflated self-esteem is to compare yourself to yourself, making a list of job duties and then ranking yourself on your ability to perform each. Drawing from the bottom half of the rank-ordered list, you can see where help is needed. This may also suggest to someone about to hire an assistant *not* to do the ordinary thing and hire a replica of himself, but to seek someone with an inverted set of skills.

As for attracting geniuses to market, Max Perkins was always looking for new writers. Most good managers are the same way—they always have job openings. Not that they lose employees, but they don't rush to fill every opening, and they keep their budgets flexible, just in case someone exceptional happens by. And having found room for an exception or two, they develop a reputation, start getting those have-I-got-a-person-for-you calls. (I've noticed that the better the manager, the less he seems to worry about budgets. I have since tumbled to the notion that this is not only because quality work justifies itself, but because the best people gravitate toward those companies that struggle to keep *up* with demand rather than *under* budget.)

PARENT IDEA

Perkins protested his fame, claiming to desire anonymity; yet he was the kind of man to whom people were attracted and became something of a celebrity.

OFFSPRING

It was by being the sort of man who befriended talented people that Max Perkins became a man worth knowing. Understanding this, Eric would also understand that there is power in being seen as a source. If he can pass around news of job openings and become an informal job placement center, he will be a man the ambitious or fearful will always be glad to hear from. If Eric takes an interest in services beyond his own specialty and suggests specialists to whom clients can turn, then Eric will become a source, a man about whom people can say, "Call Eric—if he can't do it, he'll know someone who can."

FURTHER APPLICATIONS

I call this "source" status "The Holiday Inn Effect." As you may know, Holiday Inns do not have a "No Vacancy" sign; if they don't have rooms, they refer travelers to other hotels. Thus the hotel chain has established itself as the first place to look. Many accomplished professionals have done something akin to Holiday Inn—they have turned their offices into informal libraries, shelf after shelf of information on topics related to the organization. Not only does this information provide bits for recombination, but it pulls the possessor of the facts into discussions and into planning. The young television station vice president we met earlier, Chris Roman, is such a "librarian." (Although in practice it is his assistant and secretary who do the searching of files.) When a company is contemplating a new campaign, someone must prepare a document justifying the expense. And the easiest way to prepare that document is to call Mr. Roman and ask for data. So he and his station become part of the campaign even before there is a campaign.

As with Senator Moynihan, I will cut short the Perkins exercise; it is my hope that you are by now growing impatient with watching me produce ideas, and are ready to try some of your own. Good.

I have selected two examples for you to practice on. If one or both does not awaken your imagination, do not be alarmed—I picked them because they piqued *my* imagination; if you had read the same book, you might not have given them a thought. Once you become proficient at idea evolution, however, any anecdote will set you off, a single word can send you flying.

Remember:

- Our mission is exploration; our only goal, adventure.
- You probably reached the zenith of your creativity at age five. Be childlike. Grow down. Ask "why?" again and again. Be playful.
- Don't try to stay with the original idea—roam.
- Let ideas pair up. Get out of line. Don't be too quick to get back to reality.

Example One

These two exercises come from Franklin Delano Roosevelt's life. First, I recently learned that he *began his career as a lawyer by working as an apprentice, with no salary for a year.* This was once common practice, but now it's unusual, an intriguing possibility. See what you make of it before you read on.

I hope you started considering what jobs you might want badly enough to undertake them gratis. As for specific "solutions," there are an infinite number—but for those who may have gotten stuck, I'll work through one possibility.

Why did FDR work for free? To learn from professionals. Why? That's the best education. Why? You learn by doing.

You might consider who is doing what you want to do, and how they might teach you. If, for example, your goal is to be the proprietor of a retail store, the answers are clear. Why go back to school and get a marketing degree when you could learn by doing? You could be a clerk. Better yet, you could go to the owner of a store you like and volunteer to work weekends for free in exchange for the opportunity to work with, and learn from, the owner and his staff. If you're lucky, and you're good, the store owner might eventually offer you either a full-time management position (wherein you could accelerate your learning), or even consider being a partner in your venture. (This may strike you as farfetched, but I know of two precedents among my acquaintances.)

Perhaps you don't need so thorough an education. Maybe you are presently employed by a magazine, but hanker to publish a magazine of your own. You might decide that one thing that would make you a superior publisher is to know photography from the inside, to know how photographers work and think. So you volunteer to assist a photographer on weekend shoots.

My guess is that the FDR example allowed you to contemplate unconventional education, to ask yourself where you could gain the knowledge to make you different, to make you better. If you had a better idea, I can only say, after the other Roosevelt: Bully! If you had no ideas, try the next example—I've chosen it because it offers many alternative evolutions.

Example Two

Two of FDR's innovations as governor of New York were to undertake (1) radio "classrooms" to educate the citizens of New York; and (2) a formal annual report on his activities.

Play with those, and see what you come up with.

I think most of us could benefit from the idea of distributing an annual report. It's an idea worthy of imitation. But let us not be content with imitation. Let us consider *why* Roosevelt undertook the extra work of an annual report and radio "classrooms." Both of these were, of course, a chance for free publicity, and gave him the chance to interpret events. So perhaps you began to conjecture about some of the ways you could get publicity for your work. Perhaps you thought of FDR's ability to use media and reconsidered each medium and how it might apply to your career. Perhaps you concentrated on "classrooms," and imagined yourself conducting seminars for fellow employees or for potential customers. Any of these basic answers to "why?" could have started a roll of ideas.

New Generations

After you have worked through a few books and jotted down dozens (hundreds?) of career-acceleration ideas, the next step is to take those ideas and try to pair them up, to attempt to produce new generations. This is why I suggest being quite generous with your notecards and ink as you work through the biographies you select—ideas that are not in themselves practical, perhaps even counterproductive, can still carry the seed of greatness, genius that will not appear until later generations.

By the time you have completed your original list of ideas you will be proficient at letting them run loose in your mind. The next step is to let a pair of ideas run loose together. Go through your notecards and pick out the single "best" idea, and set the card in front of you. Now take each of the other cards, one at a time, and set it beside your "best idea." See what you can do with two ideas together. Make notes. After you have worked through all of your idea cards, pick out the second-best idea and begin the pairing again.

Let's think back for a moment to our rookie account executive, Lisa. Perhaps she thought of the idea of specializing in seeking new business among down-and-out firms as the best one in her preliminary list. (You will remember that this idea was evolved from Barbara Jordan's passing out business cards at Good Hope.) She might begin her next generation of ideas by pairing "Good Hope" with the "corporate idea graveyard," and concluding that she should write a document analyzing recent corporate successes and failures, making her something of an authority on

the prerequisites for success of new corporate under-
takings.

Next, she might think of making her regular work
do "double duty." How could she advance her Good
Hope idea as part of her ordinary job assignment?
She might get herself assigned to the weakest account the agency has, making her regular work practice for her new venture. Then, she might decide to
follow Moynihan's example and, once her project
was underway, do a newsletter covering her progress. She might take the idea of selling someone
else's genius and try to find accounting or law firms
that specialize in reorganizing failing businesses, which
she might be able to interest in some kind of part-
nership. Thinking of Lombardi and scoreboards, she
could gather data on changes in advertising expendi-
tures and try to prove that turnaround businesses
have larger percentage increases in advertising spending than calm-water firms.

On and on. As I think you can see, her basic idea
of developing a new business specialty soon becomes
much more than just an idea. Lisa has the creative
wherewithal to write an entire program, a complete
proposal for implementation. Instead of an offhand,
"Hey, I think I've got a swell idea!," she will have a
major proposal to present to her major advertising
agency. And she will have done this in the first
weeks of her self-evolution. Finally, consider this:
her "Good Hope" proposal will be only one of
dozens she is developing. She will quickly establish
herself as someone to be watched, helped, given
choice assignments.

PART
THREE

Implementation

I despise patience.

RENÉ MAGRITTE

CHAPTER 5

PAINTS AND BRUSHES

---■---

You are remembered for the rules you break.

Douglas MacArthur

A romance with work and creativity on demand: these alone are the prerequisites of accomplishment. *Wait!*, you say. What about all the rest—hard work, mentors, courage, personality, not to mention luck—are these not the stuff of greatness? Of course. They are to the achiever what paints and brushes are to the artist—vital, but secondary. If a person is passionate and innovative, he or she will acquire the tools needed and the skill to use them. Without vision, without innovation, what can a person do with tools but imitate?

But still there remains the business of *implementing* ideas. Creative *thoughts* don't make a creative life. So let us reconsider the topics of a thousand self-help success tomes—luck, mentors, courage, personality, and hard work—this time in the light of passion and innovation. To do so, let us focus on those who make their lives originals, noting the ways in which they use their tools.

Luck

We begin by studying luck: let us see if we can weigh out the serendipity from the science. Take one of history's great lessons, that of the bacteriologist Alexander Fleming, who came into his lab one day to find his culture dishes of *Staphylococcus* bacteria contaminated with a green mold. Sir Alexander could have shouted *Ick!* or *Damn the luck!* and scrubbed out his dishes. Which is what hundreds of others had undoubtedly done. However, Sir Alexander was able to recognize this bit of "bad luck" as an important recombination of two familiar elements—bacteria and mold—and observe the result, that the bacteria near the fungus had disappeared, been killed. This accident was, of course, the discovery of penicillin and the birth of antibiotics. A "mountain climber" of a scientist, eager to get to the top, would have been too busy, too serious, for such a surprise. It is the mind that is out of line, out of the ruts of the minds that have preceded it, that is more likely to bump into opportunity.

But we know that good fortune need not wait upon such an accidental recombination as a contaminated culture dish. The person determined to be unique becomes a magnet for opportunity. Remember the Accomplishment Spiral—innovation reinforces itself. With that in mind let us reconsider two success stories begun earlier in this volume.

■ GENE FEIST and his Roundabout Theater in New York were "lucky enough" to get Malcolm McDowell to play the lead in what became a famous production of *Look Back in Anger* (later videotaped and shown nationally on cable television). Dissecting this luck, we see that it truly was the result of establishing the Roundabout as a place for provocative theater and thus a magnet for reviewers. When actors have something to prove to the theater world, they look for an audience of critics. Malcolm McDowell had just made the movie *Caligula*, and perhaps sought to atone for that thespian sin. At least in part, it was self-interest, not largess or coincidence, that took McDowell to the Roundabout Theater. And if Gene Feist is a lucky man, it is because his passion told him to build his theater right on the highway where luck passes.

■ WAS THE CHARM of the AT&T Building a fortunate happenstance? The architectural firm of Johnson and Burgee could be said to be lucky enough to have AT&T for a client, and lucky enough to have its chairman, John DeButts, say he wanted "something distinctive." But then again, AT&T came to Johnson and Burgee because *they had a reputation for doing distinctive work.* And how did the firm get that reputation? By exciting the imaginations of its architects with questions such as, "If it isn't going to be like a box, *what will it be like?*" Moreover, dozens of variations are experimented with, first in drawings, and then in the firm's own model shop (installed so that elements of a design can be "played with" in three dimensions). The building charms the eye because the firm long ago learned to charm the imaginations of its architects.

When we talk about the components of something complex working well together, we sometimes say they "fell into place," as if the result was a lucky roll of the dice. But when we examine the process, we see that the dice are rolled and rolled and rolled until the "lucky" result is obtained. Those who put themselves in a position to get a nearly unlimited number of rolls of the dice do not rely upon luck but upon odds, upon logic.

Where luck seems to enter the lives of achievers is in their learning to get out of line; the odds favor ordinariness. Many of the achievers I have observed did *not* make a conscious decision to be unique, but spoke of out-of-line *hardships* as their luck. One such case is that of Dr. Steven Brown, past president of the American Marketing Association, as well as a researcher, professor, author, corporate board member, and consultant. He told me:

> I'm not sure if I would have been as successful if I had not been devastated by a severe case of juvenile rheumatoid arthritis. From the seventh to the twelfth grade I never attended school full-time, and I again had severe problems in my sophomore and junior years in college. For much of this time I was in constant pain and could walk only with the aid of crutches.

Dr. Brown recognized his disease as having brought him more than the usual support from his family. (Freud, who considered himself his mother's favorite child, said that that role gave him a "conqueror's mentality.") Further, the young Steve Brown was forced to accept the impossibility of excelling in his "first ambition," to be an athlete, turning instead to intellectual pursuits. Finally, and I'm not certain if Dr. Brown is himself conscious of this fact, his disease gave him what no sports team, no school, could—training in being an exception.

Therefore, allowing for the luck that causes someone to be knocked out of line, I conclude that explorers not only put themselves in a position to be surprised, but they *expect* surprise, *demand* surprise of themselves. They acknowledge that the uncommon is forever rare, and in doing so they turn the odds in their favor, give themselves nearly infinite chances to be surprised. The passionate explorer, like a casino operator, is in the business of luck.

Mentors

I believe the recent public fascination with mentors has done almost as much to *inhibit* careers as has "positive thinking." The Great Mentor Search is nothing but a call for imitation of the most puppyish sort, a stand-in-line strategy that suggests being dragged ahead on the leash of some generous sage. I'll put my faith in self-reliance, thank you.

But does this mean there is nothing to be said for currying favor? The secret to winning the acceptance and support of your superiors is being better, being different; solve your boss's problems and you'll *both* get promoted. If you're passed over in favor of some sycophant or a seducer, get yourself to a competitive enterprise—the one you're in now is about to be toppled by a smarter competitor.

Must one then turn inward, admire no one? No! Passionate exploration is the opposite of introversion. The creative achiever is always learning, endlessly absorbing bits of genius for recombination, and often finding them in the lives and work of those who precede him. The poet John Ciardi said it to me best:

> I hope I may say that the English poets sound in my head from Beowulf through Chaucer to Shakespeare, Spenser, Donne, Milton, Pope, Byron, Keats, and many many more. A musician learns by listening enchanted to the music of the past. Not to one voice. To all the great chorus. When I was younger, in periods of intense infatuation, I sometimes imitated a particular poet. But one must be faithless. One must love them all, trying to gather the richness of all of them into one's own voice. It would be a mistake for a modern composer to write in strict imitation of Mozart. And a greater mistake not to know him as a master among many masters.

Ciardi makes it clear that one must not imitate, but rather, consciously or unconsciously, must consult the masters, listen to "the chorus."

This "chorus" of masters is not limited to artists. Don Linehan, an executive with the 3M Company, told me that he has "edited together the most wonderful parts of about ten films—the best line of the best scene, delivered perfectly." When Mr. Linehan is in need of inspiration, he turns on his videotape and bathes his mind in the traits of some of the finest characters motion pictures have presented.

Harris Mullen, former magazine publisher, now a developer, describes the hero he has created as a standard against which he assesses his performance:

> I think I always conjured up my hero and shaped him to meet the need at the time. He was always strongest where I was weakest. He was a fancy dresser. I was a sloppy dresser. He was a good dancer. I was not. He was comfortable in a crowd. I was uneasy. When I was vice-president of the sophomore class, he was the president. He was always there just a step ahead of me. Funny. When I was young he was always a few years older than I was, but when I reached 40 he began to get younger.

Indeed, such composite heroes are the norm, not the exception. While there exists among creative people and other achievers a strong respect for those with like talents, an equally strong contrarian streak precludes the notion of strict imitation. The typical case is to admire genius but not to imitate it, to add the mentor's voice to a chorus of masters.

Hard Work

Recalling how achievers tend to speak of their careers ("the quickening thing," "a turn-on," "a spiral of energy"), it isn't surprising that such careers are characterized by devotion and long hours of work.

Take, for example, Richard Mitchell—publisher of the *Underground Grammarian*, author of several books on language, and certainly the only grammarian to appear on "The Tonight Show." Dr. Mitchell says that in his profession not only is it "very easy to coast," but that a tenured professor can "disappear." But he does the opposite: "My daughter speaks of me as working under a curse the way the Flying Dutchman sails under a curse. I just can't stop." Is Richard Mitchell a workaholic? I suppose so. What achiever isn't? Indeed, he told me that the worst thing that could happen to him would be to get rich, for a rich man might work less. He explained that he had grown up in a wealthy family and found that "it's not a productive life." He has asked himself, "Could a wealthy man do the things I do?" The *Underground Grammarian* reflects Dr. Mitchell's attention to detail and careful work. "It's composed with the most incredible slowness. If I became wealthy, I'd stop doing that and the thing wouldn't be good anymore. This is why I'd never buy a lottery ticket."

Such dedication admits the possibility of conflicts between career and personal life. The most common adjustments are to sacrifice idle pleasures for professional ones—less time watching television, less sleep, less fishing or golf, more travel, a greater number of social and professional engagements, more evenings spent in background reading. But for true achievers, work is both a great joy and a source of energy. Many such men and women could, if they wanted to, work far less than they do, or not work at all—but the same insatiable curiosity that brought them their success causes them to remain restless, to take on new projects, to have a multiplicity of interests. Is a devotion to work selfish? The psychologist Gene Ruyle has written, "Reaching forth to take life in one's own hands and use it is the most rudimentary expression of self-worth a human being is capable of; and it is the very opposite of selfishness (which always isolates), because this movement of life brings one into more contact with everything and everyone, not less." Passionate work flows from neither greed nor selfishness. The old bromides on "too much work and not enough play" may apply to a worker stuck in a rut, but it is a meaningless distinction to those who play while they work. For such workers, the more work they do, the more lively, interesting, entertained, and entertaining they are.

Courage

There is no question but that innovation demands courage. But ask innovators if they are especially brave, and most will cough or snort or snicker. More than one achiever I have known has confessed to being fleet in escaping physical danger. Yet they all were able to push themselves over anxieties that would have cowed an average person. This bravery appears to spring not from the heart of the person but the heart of the enterprise—these individuals simply were so persuaded about their tasks that anxieties were either accepted or swept aside. What, for instance, would you make of a man who is so anxious about his work, and so yellow about doing it, that he throws up on the way to his job? When we know that such a man was football coach Bear Bryant, who "used to have a regular stop on my way from the office to upchuck before a game," we can learn something important about courage. Anxiety is one measure of risk, and thus it is the explorer's companion. Many achievers have said they welcome anxiety, recognizing it as a measure of risk and, hence, potential for progress, and inviting the "adrenaline high" it provides. I'd like to consider two sorts of courage separately—performance courage and responsibility courage.

Performance Courage

Those who seek to be different grow used to being stared at. Society is fascinated by those who are not fascinated by it. Moreover, an ability to forcefully express one's opinions is typically essential to success. I call this "acting," although the word offends some, perhaps because it suggests phoniness, and the passionate achiever despises insincerity. Read what the following achievers have to say about this type of acting:

> *Paul del Rossi, president of GCC Cinemas*: "Sometimes people will say to me, 'What do you do in your job, Paul?' and I say, 'I play Knute Rockne.'

Part of my job is to make people believe in themselves. But you can't tap dance. You can't fool people. When I'm playing Knute Rockne, I feel like Knute Rockne."

Bob DeVito, one of the country's leading graphic-industrial designers: "I bring information into a context in which I can express it as well and clearly and dramatically as possible. Is that acting? It is life force. Everyone performs an act of life. If you express yourselves with beautiful words or drawings or expressions, you are lively. There is nothing insincere about it."

When the work matters, there is no need for artificial passion, not even a need for "psyching up." If anything, the opposite is true—the battle may be with an *excess* of caring, with anxiety. We will deal with this extensively in the next chapter, but for now let me say that anxiety is overcome by commitment to the enterprise. Three men who are accustomed to appearing in front of audiences had this to say:

Cellist Christopher Rex: "Every time I perform a solo I must contend with anxiety. I don't wish to rid myself totally of this stress because it is partially responsible for needed adrenaline. But I can control it to a large extent by realizing why I'm a musician. God has given me musical talent in order to communicate beauty and ideals to others. If I perform with that purpose in mind, rather than with the intent of increasing the audience's opinion of my talents and ability, then the anxiety is diminished."

Advertising executive Roger Myers, who must continually do presentations to his agency's clients and prospects: "If anxiety is there, I respond to it. If it isn't, I create it. You can't concentrate on walking a tightrope unless there is a clear and present danger that you might fall off."

Alejandro Menendez, formerly principal male dancer, Nuevo Mundo Ballet of Venezuela: "I never let myself think about anything but the dance. I think only of the music, the steps, the grandeur of the ballet. I lose myself. The audience disappears. I disappear. There is only the dance."

Responsibility Courage

There is another kind of courage, what I think of as the "Patton Effect," the willingness to take on difficult tasks and endure criticism. An often-neglected truth is that to win is to cause others to lose. For example, Hugh McColl, chairman and president of the banking chain NCNB, said, "We don't honor historical monopolies. Just because someone has been in the market for a hundred years and they are good ol' boys doesn't mean it's their territory. We didn't get to be the largest bank in the Southeast by holding our relative position." This, he realizes, would be called "predatory" by some, but one reason Mr. McColl has been so successful is his willingness to topple old ways, including the unwritten codes of the banking business. "There are banks that won't consider financing a hostile takeover. My reaction is, hostile to whom? What may be hostile to management could be beneficial to shareholders."

Hugh McColl is not alone in making enemies—resentments are, of course, not limited to the business world, but shadow the successful wherever they go. Because it is the nature of the accomplishing individual to take risks, to get out of line, it is also the nature of accomplishment to create resentments and hostilities. Indeed, many achievers learn to welcome hostility. Richard Mitchell publishes in his *Underground Grammarian* examples of poor writing, and the poor thinking that invariably produces it, naming names and mercilessly mocking the offenders. His mission—reform of the educational system in this country (my words, not his)—is simply too important for him to be concerned with injured feelings. He told me, "Every time someone says, 'We do have to be practical,' or, 'We have to be realistic,' something shameful follows." Later, he added, "I am not a courageous person. But, damn it, where the work of my mind is concerned, I'm going to have confidence in it until somebody shows me I'm wrong. Nobody can show me by insult or anger I'm wrong. But if someone can show me by thought that I'm wrong, by God, I'm wrong. But that's no disgrace. What's a disgrace is to be hypocritical or a copycat."

Dr. Mitchell may not be "a courageous person" yet he is willing to take risks, risks of sufficient consequence that, he says, "there was a time when I checked underneath the car for wires."

Notice the irony operating here: being unique is grounds for admiration, ostracism, or both. The majority—that is to say, the unexceptional—want everyone to be a winner. Or, to reflect the majority mentality more correctly, to prevent anyone from losing. Many of the corporations I work with have, like public schools, "quality-controlled" themselves into mediocrity. Large companies tend to become places where employees learn to *think small*. Corporations react to mediocrity by narrowing job functions and instituting vast systems of checking and double-checking. As jobs narrow, so do the minds attracted to them. The downward spiral ends with a labyrinth of expensive clerks who know more about what their job is *not* than what it *is*. I don't believe the "Peter Principle" operates in many large corporations; they've overcome it by making job tasks so routine that anyone can do them properly. Incompetence becomes as rare as excellence. Such large companies don't ask too much of their managerial employees, they ask too little. Little feet fill little shoes.

But this discussion soon takes us back, as all things in this book do, to the romance with a job. If you have found a career to which you are devoted, you are unlikely to be plagued with doubts about the fundamental worth of your enterprise. If you are convinced of the grandeur of your endeavor, you are less likely to be troubled by the unfairness of your success, for personal achievement lies in advancing the interest of an enterprise already deemed worthy.

Luck, mentors, hard work, courage: look to career success, and you will see these elements. Look to ambitious mediocrity, and what do you see there? Luck, mentors, hard work, courage. Both true and untrue artists own these paints and brushes. Only when luck, mentors, hard work, and courage are the tools of a *passion* do they take on a synergy, a grace that makes it seem as if angels sit on the achiever's shoulder.

CHAPTER 6

STRIKING MATCHES

I am wealthy in my friends.

William Shakespeare

W hat force is capable of thwarting a passionate worker who possesses an endless supply of innovations? What superhuman power can knock the mind of the self-reliant achiever back into line? The clichés a person carries within, the relentless inertia of the past. Like the pebble that causes a horse to go lame, tiny self-perceptions can hobble a career. We've covered some of these already: "This too shall pass." "Quitters never win." "Let's be practical." "If I were a rich man." Yet as worthless as these coins of mediocrity are, there is one even worse, one that picks accomplishment's pocket: "That's just the way I am."

W. C. Fields used to say he pitied the man who woke up without a hangover, for that man knew he wouldn't feel better all day. Well, I pity those who boast or moan, "I am what I am"—the speaker has abandoned his future to the coincidences of his past. If you don't believe in change, you can't believe in progress. Before you fill your knapsack with ideas and set out on your career exploration, let's make sure you've emptied the psychological pebbles out of your boots. I don't want some little half-hidden belief like "I'm basically shy," or "That's not my style," or "If only I knew the right people" to send you limping back into line.

Connections

The closest I ever came to drowning was in a small cove of Lake Lanier in northern Georgia. My companion developed a cramp, took in water, panicked. Attempting a rescue, I was repeatedly dragged beneath the surface until I too was gasping and exhausted. With the slow-motion clarity of vision of an endangered man, I turned to the shore, only a short distance away, and saw there a half a dozen men standing on a dock, chatting. I could have called to them, but I didn't. Instead I struggled, risking two lives, floundering till we happened to strike a buoy.

When I recounted this misadventure to a professor friend, she seemed not at all surprised. She told me about research demonstrating that such silence was not uncommon among those who were the victims of an accident or criminal assault or other emergency that endangered their lives. Case studies proved that this silence was not simply being struck dumb with fear (some of those interviewed had spoken during their crises), but some deep unwillingness to call for assistance. Apparently the silence was an excess of courtesy, a "triumph" of politeness. I knew then that I had almost drowned *in a sea of misplaced civility*.

So it may be with your career—you can see those who could help you, they walk in the sun up there on the shore, but you fail to call out to them.

Remember the moment in the classic film *The Graduate*, when Benjamin, fresh from college, was pulled aside at a party by one of his parents' friends and offered in reverent tones advice that would change his life? The unctuous sage whispered The Secret, just one word: "Plastics." If I could whisper one word into your ear right now, I would whisper, "Connections."

Most of you will agree that there are individuals who could, if they so chose, accelerate your career. "If only I knew them!" you might say, wishing your father had befriended the successful or that you had gone to a better school. The truth is, you *do* know the right people, you just haven't met them. You have many friends you haven't met, indirect ones— friends of friends and friends of friends of friends. Let us stop to consider the pioneering research of Stanley Milgram and what he called the "small world" phenomenon.

Milgram, a social researcher, has conducted a fascinating investigation into what he calls the "small world problem." He observed the networks of friends and relatives and wondered if it were possible for a specific individual in one part of the country to get an introduction to another specific individual in another part, using only "friends" as contacts. ("Friends" being defined as persons known on a first-name basis.)

Could a letter be passed via "friends" from a randomly selected individual in Nebraska to some other random person in Boston? Not only was the answer yes, but it took surprisingly few intermediaries to accomplish the task. It typically took five or six people (5.5 persons) for two individuals half a continent apart to communicate through a chain of acquaintances.

Say you want to sit down and discuss a career with someone successful in it. You could just get on the phone and ask people in that career to meet with you. To do so works well if you are comfortable calling strangers *and* can get the names and numbers you need *and* you can overcome the natural reticence of those you meet to open up to an out-of-the-blue stranger. An alternative is to tap into the grapevine of friends, and friends[2] (that is, friends of friends), and friends[3] (friends of friends of friends), and so on.

If you know just 50 people on a first-name basis, and so do all the people you know, you have 2,500 friends of friends, and 125,000 friends of friends of friends, and over 6,000,000 friends of friends of friends of friends. You have contacts! (Naturally there would be some overlap, so the exact number would be smaller.)

You want to meet someone in a specialized career, say, someone who does the TV weather. You don't know any weatherpeople, but you do know someone who sells equipment to a television station. You ask that friend if he knows any weatherpeople. He doesn't, but he gives you the names of two people with whom he works at the television station. You call one and he switches you over to the weatherperson, who is glad to talk to you because you came via a trusted co-worker. By agreeing to have lunch with you, the weatherperson is not only helping you, but helping a co-worker.

If you didn't know someone in electronics, you might have thought of someone who works for a company that advertises on local television and started your chain that way. There are many possible chains. Remember, the object is to get closer to the people you want to meet with each contact, and not to limit your conception of contacts to those you know personally.

But getting introductions is not always the sole obstacle—making use of contacts is, at first, difficult. Many people I've talked to consider having contacts essential to their work, and are so accustomed to calling and meeting associates that it no longer provokes anxiety. However, most could recall a time when their phone-hand was sweaty of palm. The best description I have found of this "contact anxiety" appeared in an advice-for-young-novelists article by Diane Lefer:

> You may think you have no contacts, but maybe you're not defining the word correctly. To me, "contact" used to mean someone I felt comfortable about approaching—a definition that tended to exclude anyone in a position of power or authority.
>
> When I found myself with a completed novel and no agent, I psyched myself up to get in touch with agents and editors I'd met or who had shown interest in my work in the past. The whole idea of saying, "You don't remember me,

but ten years ago . . ." made me feel like a poor relation.

The denouement of Ms. Lefer's story is that she made those calls and wrote those letters, with this result: "Much to my delight, the people I called and wrote to did remember me and were very willing to read my manuscript. In fact, I learned that once editors express interest in your work, it's actually rude not to get back in touch when you have something new."

You might still be skeptical: Why would some shiny-shoes VIP help little ol' me?, you say.

To answer that, let us consider why people do anything. Listing common human desires is a familiar challenge. The "basic urges" for physical necessities, happiness, fulfillment, sex, security and recognition usually compose the list. These are the overriding themes of humanity and are too encompassing to be of practical use for fast connections. A more detailed list of common human desires has been developed by the Direct Mail Advertising Association (the association of those who find out which appeals motivate people every time they send out a mailing):

> to save time
> to avoid effort
> for comfort
> to gratify curiosity
> for cleanliness
> for health
> to escape physical or mental pain

for praise
for enjoyment or happiness
to be popular
to attract the opposite sex
to take advantage of opportunity
to be in style
to satisfy appetite
to emulate others
to make money
to save money
to protect reputation
to conserve possessions
to protect family
for beautiful possessions
for safety
to avoid criticism
to be individual
to avoid trouble

Which of these basic motivations might apply to helping you? Assisting you won't take much time, will be enjoyable, might satisfy curiosity, could protect a reputation as a "nice guy," will avoid criticism by the mutual friend "connection," and so on. You'll end up saying, "I'm practically doing the guy a favor by asking for his help!" And you might be doing just that. The achievers I interviewed were both curious and opinionated; they welcomed questions. Moreover, they themselves often called upon others for help and might just make use of a stranger for ideas or reactions to ideas.

Remember Gene Ruyle's assertion that hard work is the opposite of selfishness, that work brings "one more into contact with everyone and everything"?

Making and keeping contacts becomes a joy of the passionate worker. Davis Masten, president of the consulting firm of Cheskin + Masten, told me, "I stay in touch with people from all phases of my life, with far more people that I need to from a strict P. and L. [profit and loss] standpoint. If I don't have anything to do some afternoon, or don't feel like working, I'll get on the phone. Other people go pay a therapist, I call someone I haven't talked to in months—that's the best upper."

Performing

All of us are actors—some of us are just better actors than others. Think about how you came to be the actor that you are now. As a child by imitating your parents and peers, adding whatever child's emotions you felt. Sometime, somewhere, you learned how to act. There is nothing mystical or sacred about it— what you learned was the result of the coincidences of time and place. The emotions and actions you learned as a child may be no more appropriate today than are the clothes you wore at age ten.

If you refuse to think of yourself as an actor—if you think that such a label implies phoniness or artificiality—you are probably foregoing the opportunity to become skillful at expressing yourself and evoking strong responses in others. As for any "phoniness" or "artificiality" in being an actor, it was the greatest insight of the world's greatest director, Stanislavski, that fine acting is never insincere. The best actors develop a facility for feeling emotion and then conveying it, as this delightful passage from *An Actor Prepares* should make clear:

"Let us give a new play," said the Director to Maria, as he came into the classroom today.

"Here is the gist of it: your mother has lost her job and her income; she has nothing to sell to pay for your tuition in dramatic school. In consequence you will be obliged to leave tomorrow. But a friend has come to your rescue. She has no cash to lend you, so she has brought you a brooch set in valuable stones. Her generous act has moved and excited you. Can you accept such a sacrifice? You cannot make up your mind. You try to refuse. Your friend sticks the pin into a curtain and walks out. You follow her into the corridor, where there is a long scene of persuasion, refusal, tears, gratitude. In the end you accept, your friend leaves, and you come back into the room to get the brooch. But—where is it? Can anyone have entered and taken it? In a rooming house that would be altogether possible. A careful, nerve-racking search ensues.

"Go up on the stage. I shall stick the pin in a fold of this curtain and you are to find it."

In a moment he announced that he was ready.

Maria dashed onto the stage as if she had been chased. She ran to the edge of the footlights and then back again, holding her head with both hands, and writhing with terror. Then she came forward again, and then again went away, this time in the opposite direction. Rushing out toward the front she seized the folds of the curtain and shook them desperately, finally

179

burying her head in them. This act she intended to represent looking for the brooch. Not finding it, she turned quickly and dashed off the stage, alternately holding her head or beating her breast, apparently to represent the general tragedy of the situation.

Those of us who were sitting in the orchestra could scarcely keep from laughing.

It was not long before Maria came running down to us in a most triumphant manner. Her eyes shone, her cheeks flamed.

"How do you feel?" asked the Director.

"Oh, just wonderful! I can't tell you how wonderful. I'm so happy," she cried, hopping around on her seat. "I feel just as if I had made my debut . . . really at home on the stage."

"That's fine," said he encouragingly, "but where is the brooch? Give it to me."

"Oh, yes," said she, "I forgot that."

"That is rather strange. You were looking hard for it, and you forgot it!"

We could scarcely look around before she was up on the stage again, and was going through the folds of the curtain.

"Do not forget this one thing," said the Director warningly, "if the brooch is found you are saved. You may continue to come to these classes. But if the pin is not found you will have to leave the school."

Immediately her face became intense. She glued her eyes on the curtain, and went over every fold of the material from top to bottom, painstakingly, systematically. This time her search was at a much slower pace, but we were all sure that she was not wasting a second of her time and that she was sincerely excited, although she made no effort to seem so.

"Oh, where is it? Oh, I've lost it."

This time the words were muttered in a low voice.

"It isn't there," she cried, with despair and consternation, when she had gone through every fold.

Her face was all worry and sadness. She stood motionless as if her thoughts were far away. It was easy to feel how the loss of the pin had moved her.

We watched, and held our breath.

Finally the Director spoke.

"How do you feel now, after your second search?" he asked.

"How do I feel? I don't know." Her whole manner was languid, she shrugged her shoulders as she tried for some answer, and unconsciously her eyes were still on the floor of the stage. "I looked hard," she went on, after a moment.

"That's true. This time you really did look," said he. "But what did you do the first time?"

"Oh, the first time I was excited, I suffered."

"Which feeling was more agreeable, the first, when you rushed about and tore up the curtain, or the second, when you searched through it quietly?"

"Why, of course, the first time, when I was looking for the pin."

"No, do not try to make us believe that the first time you were looking for the pin," said he. "You did not even think of it. You merely sought to suffer, for the sake of suffering.

"But the second time you really did look. We all saw it; we understood, we believed, because your consternation and distraction actually existed.

"Your first search was bad. The second was good."

I think you can see how genuine actions based upon feelings differ greatly from "acting," or as Stanislavski calls it, "mechanical acting." I suspect we have all met individuals who mechanically act their roles in life, trying to play a part with all the cliché actions. Who hasn't met salesmen who were mechanically acting like salesmen?

Perhaps you have observed that the best salesmen never "act like salesmen." Just as the best professors do not "act like professors," the best writers do not "act like writers," and so on. The best are always different and unique—you know that. In Stanislavski's words, "Clichés will fill up every empty spot in a role which is not already solid with living feeling."

Stanislavski also urges actors to be "merciless" in cutting out every tendency toward mechanical acting. He was fond of saying, sometimes in a bellow, sometimes in a whisper, "Cut 90 percent!" When an actor undertakes a new role, there is a tendency to vastly overact, to give a part ten times the acting that is necessary. "When in doubt, leave it out," as Count Basie used to say.

Emotion Memory

So we know we must not overact; we do this by denying ourselves mechanical actions and clichés. Like the girl searching for the brooch, we must let our feelings guide our actions. But how to develop "right" feelings?

Here is where you put "emotion memory" to work. One advantage of having completed the exercises back in Chapter 2, the explorations of your future self, is having a clear picture of what sort of person you are becoming. If you can feel your future self then you have some sense of the character you will play.

To make sure your feelings are genuine and not just mechanical, put your imagination in reverse; recollect those instances when you were at your finest and acted in a manner suited to your future. Recall moments from your life when you were fully in control and acted the way you would like to act. Close your eyes and transport yourself back to that day and feel those feelings anew. Capture them in your "emotion memory," and carry them with you to the present.

You might also envision moments in which someone else acted in just the way you would have liked to act in that situation. Put yourself inside them, try to feel what they must have felt. Store this in your emotion memory as well. Soon you will have a library of keenly felt emotions, and when you are tired or surly or frightened you can reach up onto your mental shelf of stored emotions and replace your negative mood with an admirable one.

Picture yourself sitting outside the door of the office of some "intimidating" person. What do you think about as you wait? In the past you probably thought about how nervous you were, about how the sweat was running down your sides, how you hoped your voice wouldn't crack, how you prayed that the person you were to meet would be nice to you. Such thoughts make you tense as a jackrabbit, and your anxiety will be communicated in your actions—no matter how hard you "act."

Consider the advantages of using the moments outside the office to bathe your consciousness in past triumphs, to think about those situations when you handled someone smoothly, or those occasions when someone you know gracefully handled a situation such as you are about to encounter. You concentrate not on the words that were spoken, but the feelings that were felt. By the time the office door swings open, you are radiating the assurance that you are at your best. Such an approach gives new meaning to the phrase "feeling your best."

Don't wait until you have an "initimidating" appointment to begin working on your emotion memory. If you are to become a skilled actor, you must develop the facility for exercising emotion memory and let those feelings dictate your actions. You must rehearse. During the next five meetings you attend, or your next five phone calls, try to be aware of the feelings of a different person each time. You might take five people from your past (say, your minister, high-school coach, a professor, your doctor, and your mother). For each one, picture them, try to feel what they must have felt when they were at their best, and then try to let those feelings guide your actions.

(Naturally, you are *not* interested here in trying to imitate their voices or their walks, although your speech patterns and actions may well reflect some of what you are feeling.)

Once you know your character, once you feel him or her inside you, you are ready for your first performance. If you are challenging yourself, forcing yourself to call or visit people you wouldn't normally confront, you might feel some nervousness. After all, this is your career. Of course, as an explorer and idea rancher, no *one* meeting will be your "only chance"—you have so many approaches to success. But atop this foundation of confidence may be some hesitation, some jitters about meeting new people or asking for help.

Such tension can undermine your performance; anxiety tends to interrupt the flow of both muscles and ideas, preventing you from putting on your best show. (Stanislavski, who taught by example, tells the story of asking a strong young man to lift one corner of a grand piano and then asking him questions. Even though the questions were not so difficult as to be taxing under normal circumstances, the student was unable to respond while supporting a part of the piano. Finally, when asked one fairly routine question, the student said, "Let me put this down and I'll tell you." This demonstrates how much of our mental capacity can be occupied by physical exertion.)

Any form of fear tends to throw the brain and body into the "fight-or-flight" syndrome, which increases sensory input and directs oxygen, and attention, to the muscles. Even more so than an actor, who has written dialogue to depend upon, you must have the resources to do the intellectual work of writing your script as you go.

How, then, to conquer tension? You probably have read one or more of the hundreds of books and articles on this subject—meditation, self-hypnosis, deep-breathing, exercise. But a Stanislavski-school actor has a great advantage over those using such techniques: he or she is capable of emotion memory and thus has the ability to recall those instances of scoffing at anxiety and performing with grace under pressure. If you have learned to recall feeling on cue, you can simply feel your way out of anxiety and into the confident personality you are assuming. Your emotion memory can turn nervous energy into radiance. You will believe that "butterflies" are natural and then let go of the thought of them, letting the heightened awareness be recycled into your performance.

Many achievers I've met had moments in their careers of either insight or triumph that served as an intellectual worry stone, moments that could be recalled with a relaxing smile and shake of the head. When about to give a speech, they are not filling themselves with self-doubt but mentally stroking an amulet such as this:

> *Harris Mullen, developer:* "I probably made 300 speeches during my career and they all made me nervous. The better prepared I was the less nervous I was. I would make myself less nervous by trying to remember something I firmly believe: your audience is not nearly so critical of what you have to say as how long it takes you to say it. Most every 15-minute speech is a success, and most 45-minute ones are failures.

"I was speaking to a group of corporate heads at Walt Disney World from a prepared text. When I reached for the last page (in the middle of a paragraph), I discovered it was missing. Since I knew I was caught, I hammed it up a bit, looking under the rostrum, in my wife's pocketbook, etcetera. The laughter grew the longer I searched and finally I took the mike and said, 'Well, you've heard enough of this, anyway.' It was the biggest applause I ever got, then or since."

This is the stuff of emotion memory; even "disasters" become cherished tales.

But, above all, the source of calm before a speech or meeting is a passion for the work. Here is John Ciardi on reaching an audience:

I have never had myself to sell to an audience; only the subject. Committed to a sense of its importance to me, I have never made speeches but only talked about what mattered to me that I believed mattered to those who had come to hear.

The passion. As always, the passion.

That's it. I've told you what I have to say as succinctly and clearly and objectively as I can say it. Allow me one final presentation of the lessons I hold most dear:

Achievers are:

- Self-reliant. They know that one cannot be better except by being different. (Ask enough people their opinion and they will, on average, recommend being average.)

- Explorers, not mountain climbers. The goal of the achiever is not to conquer a mountain but to fall in love with it, to be conquered by it.

- Happy malcontents. The achiever is forever asking the question, "Is there a better way?"

- Riders on the Accomplishment Spiral. They depend on self-reliance and passion to produce energy, commitment, and courage, which in turn produce innovation, accomplishment, and renewed passion.

- Men and women not of wealth, but *wealths.* Money is a convenience, not an obsession, for the ego is fed on accomplishment, not ostentation.

- Above all else, creators. Achievers know that creativity comes not from sitting alone in the dark but from just the opposite, from being out in the world, from finding bits of genius to put into combination with ordinary problems. Exploration, malcontentment, the search for a better way; the achiever listens to the chorus of accomplishments past but hears original melodies.

In sum, the achiever is a mind and a career out-of-line.

I would ask you to join me today in a solemn refusal to accept that our generation is an experiment that failed.

But, yes, know that we *are* failing.

This was once a nation of explorers, of experimenters. Adventure is in our blood . . . or *was*. How did we decide to be so patient, so safe? Eavesdrop upon our brightest young men and women and hear what preoccupies their minds: tax shelters, bottom lines, status reports. The devil gave us these. What will exorcise the bookkeeper mentality are adventure and mistakes. Here is nature's great secret: In difference there is progress. The speed of evolution is dependent upon the rate of differences, upon the willingness to make mistakes. Get out of line. Run. Take chances, or you might as well be dead.

BIBLIOGRAPHY

───────────■───────────

Aronson, Elliot. "The Rationalizing Animal." *Psychology Today*, 6 (1973): 46–52.

Berg, Scott A. *Max Perkins: Editor of Genius*. New York: E. P. Dutton, 1978.

Berlew, David E. "Leadership and Organizational Excitement." From Kolb, Rubin and McIntyre, *Organizational Psychology: A Book of Readings*. Englewood Cliffs, New Jersey: Prentice-Hall, Inc., 1974.

Bruccoli, Matthew J. (editor). *The Notebooks of F. Scott Fitzgerald*. New York: Harcourt Brace Jovanovich, 1978.

Blanchard, Kenneth, and Spencer Johnson. *The One-Minute Manager*. New York: William Morrow & Company, 1982.

Ciardi, John. "See All Evil." *The Writer*, 93 (6) (1980): 15–17.

Ciardi, John. *This Strangest Everything*. New Brunswick, New Jersey: Rutgers University Press, 1966.

Clark, Ronald W. *Freud: The Man and the Cause*. New York: Random House, 1980.

Dauten, Dale A. *Quitting*. New York: Walker & Company, 1980.

Dowling, William F. "Conversation with B. F. Skinner." *Organizational Dynamics*, Winter, 1973: 31–40.

Edwards, Betty. *Drawing on the Right Side of the Brain*. New York: J. P. Tarcher, 1979.

Flynn, George. *The Vince Lombardi Scrapbook*. New York: Grosset & Dunlap, 1976.

Fussell, Paul. *Class*. New York: Summit Books, 1983.

Galbraith, John Kenneth. *A Life in Our Times*. Boston: Houghton Mifflin Company, 1981.

Galbraith, John Kenneth. *The Anatomy of Power*. Boston: Houghton Mifflin Company, 1983.

Gissen, Jay, with Richard Behar. "The Forbes 400." *Forbes*, 132 (9) (1983): 71–159.

Goldberger, Paul. "Romanticism Is the New Motif in Architecture." *The New York Times*, October 23, 1983: 1, 35.

Hacker, Andrew. "What the Very Rich Really Think." *Forbes*, 132 (9) (1983): 66–70.

Hackman, Richard J., Greg Oldham, Robert Janson, and Kenneth Purdy. "A New Strategy for Job Enrichment." *California Management Review*, 17 (4) (1975): 58–76.

Harrison, Gilbert A. *The Enthusiast: A Life of Thornton Wilder*. New Haven and New York: Ticknor & Fields, 1983.

Hayman, Ronald. *Nietzsche: A Critical Life*. New York: Oxford University Press, 1980.

Jordan, Barbara, and Shelby Hearon. *Barbara Jordan: A Self-Portrait*. New York: Doubleday & Company, 1979.

Katerberg, Ralph, and Gary J. Blau. "An Examination of Level and Direction of Effort and Job Performance." *Academy of Management Journal*, 26 (2) (1983): 249–257.

Koberg, Don, and Jim Bagnall. *The Universal Traveler*. Los Altos, California: William Kaufmann, Inc., 1972.

Lasch, Christopher. *The Culture of Narcissism*. New York: W. W. Norton & Company Inc., 1978.

Lefer, Diane. "Trade Secrets." *The Writer*, 96 (12) (1983): 12–15.

BIBLIOGRAPHY

Manchester, William. *American Caesar: Douglas MacArthur*. Boston: Little, Brown & Company, 1978.

Masson, Jeffrey Moussaieff. *The Assault on Truth*. New York: Farrar, Straus and Giroux, 1984.

Maugham, W. Somerset. *The Summing Up*. New York: The Literary Guild of America, Inc., 1938.

"Men and Their Machines." *M Magazine*, 1 (8) (1984).

Milgram, Stanley. *The Individual in a Social World*. Reading, Mass.: Addison-Wesley Publishing Company, 1977.

Miller, Jonathan. *States of Mind*. New York: Pantheon Books, 1983.

Mitchell, Arnold. "Changing Values and Lifestyles." SRI International, unpublished paper, (1979): 1–22.

Mitchell, Richard. *Less Than Words Can Say*. Boston: Little, Brown & Company, 1979.

Mitchell, Richard. *The Graves of Academe*. Boston: Little, Brown & Company, 1981.

Moynihan, Daniel Patrick. *A Dangerous Place*. Boston: Little, Brown & Company, 1978.

Myers, David G. *The Inflated Self*. New York: The Seabury Press, 1980.

Myers, Roger. "What Do Those Pitches in New Business Presentations Really Mean?" *Advertising Age*, 54 (37) (1983): 34.

Palau i Fabre, Josep. *Picasso: The Early Years 1881–1907*. New York: Rizzoli, 1981.

Penrose, Roland. *Picasso: His Life and Work*. Berkeley: University of California Press, 1981.

Peter, Laurence J., and Raymond Hall. *The Peter Principle*. New York: William Morrow & Company, Inc., 1969.

Peters, Thomas J., and Robert H. Waterman, Jr. *In Search of Excellence*. New York: Harper & Row, 1982.

Ruyle, Jean. *Making a Life*. New York: The Seabury Press, 1983.

Simon, John. *Paradigms Lost*. New York: Clarkson & Potter, Inc., 1980.

Skinner, B. F. *Beyond Freedom and Dignity*. New York: Alfred A. Knopf, Inc., 1971.

Stanislavski, Constantin. *An Actor Prepares*. New York: Theatre Arts Books, 1936.

Stanton, Robert J., and Gore Vidal (editors). *Views from a Window*. Seacaucus, New Jersey: Lyle Stuart Inc., 1980.

Staw, Barry M. *Intrinsic and Extrinsic Motivation*. Morristown, New Jersey: General Learning Press, 1976.

Toffler, Alvin. *Future Shock*. New York: Random House, 1970.

Vidal, Gore. *Matters of Fact and of Fiction*. New York: Random House, 1977.

Waters, John. *Shock Value*. New York: Dell Publishing Co., Inc., 1981.